Vintage Style Crochet Projects

Agnieszka Strycharska

TUVA

Tuva Publishing

www.tuvapublishing.com

Address: Merkez Mah. Cavusbasi Cad. No:71
Cekmekoy - Istanbul 34782 / Turkey
Tel: +9 0216 642 62 62

Vintage Style Crochet Projects

First Print: 2015 / June

All Global Copyrights Belongs To

Tuva Tekstil ve Yayıncılık Ltd

Content: Crochet

Editor in Chief: Ayhan DEMİRPEHLİVAN
Project Editor: Kader DEMİRPEHLİVAN
Designer: Agnieszka STRYCHARSKA
Technical Editor: Michelle ROBINSON, K. Leyla ARAS, Büşra ESER
Assistant: Zilal ÖNEL
Graphic Design: Ömer ALP, Abdullah BAYRAKÇI
Photography: Agnieszka STRYCHARSKA, Tuva Publishing

ISBN: 978-605-9192-00-2

Printing House
Bilnet Matbaacılık ve Yayıncılık A.Ş.

TuvaYayincilik   TuvaPublishing
TuvaYayincilik   TuvaPublishing

Contents

5

Introduction

My mum first taught me to crochet with a few simple stitches when I was 10 years old. I could crochet a simple flower but I didn't have any patience for it back then and preferred painting instead.

So, for years I forgot about crochet and finished art school in Poland. After art school I went on to work in theatre and films making decorations for plays and movies. In my spare time I enjoyed painting in oils and acrylics on canvas After the birth of my daughters I no longer had time or space for my paintings and easel. I needed a hobby that would make me as happy as painting did but also something that was clean and easy to hide away. Crochet was the perfect solution so I replaced my paintbrushes for hooks.

I couldn't remember any of my mum's first crochet lessons so I had to learn over again. I started by looking a photos and reproducing the project from what I could see. One day I realized that I love crochet more than painting and it has become a very important part of my life. Now I crochet every day! I love to design patterns for my family and also for magazines all over the world. I have fun designing and get much happiness from the process too.

Using color in my work is very important to me also. It gives me energy and puts a smile on my face. I love to be surrounded by colorful crochet all around my home and in my garden too. I love it when my home is bright and happy! I also love to wear colorful and unique crochet accessories like mittens, scarves and bags.

I share my work on my blog **niebieskachata.blogspot.com** and now in this book also.

I hope that this book will be an inspiration to you and that making the projects in this book will make your home a happy and colorful place. I would like to dedicate this book to my mother Teresa and thank her for all her love, support and those first crochet lessons. I also want to thank my husband and especially my daughters, Sophie and Mary, for all their help and hard work as models for this book.

Projects

Star Potholder

Blue Flower Potholder

African Flower Potholder

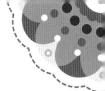

Star Potholder

Materials

Hook: 3.5 mm

DMC Natura Just Cotton: 50g-115m

Colors:
- N 83   Blé
- N 06   Rose Layette
- N 25   Aguamarina
- N 32   Rose Soraya
- N 30   Glicine
- N 05   Bleu Layette

Finished size: 20 cm diameter

dc - double crochet

ch - chain

sc - single crochet

ss - slip stitch

Base Round: Using Rose Layette, ch 4, join with a ss into first ch to make a ring.

ROUND 1: Working into ring, ch 3 (counts as first dc), 1 dc, ch 1, * 2 dc, ch 1. Repeat from * 7 more times. Join with a ss into top of beginning ch-3. Fasten off. (9 sets of 2-dc and 9 x ch-1 sps)

ROUND 2: Join Aguamarina into first ch-1 sp, ch 3 (counts as first dc), 1 dc into same sp, ch 2. *2 dc into next sp, ch 2. Repeat from * to end. Join with a ss into top of beginning ch-3. Fasten off.

ROUND 3: Join Rose Soraya into first ch-2 sp, [ch 3 (counts as first dc), 1 dc, ch 3, 2 dc] into same sp, ch 1, * (2 dc, ch 3, 2 dc) into next sp, ch 1. Repeat from * to end. Join with a ss into top of beginning ch-3. Fasten off.

ROUND 4: Join Glicine into first ch-3 sp, [ch 3 (counts as first dc), 2 dc, ch 3, 3 dc] into same sp, ch 1, * (3 dc, ch 3, 3 dc) into next ch-3 sp, ch 1, skip next ch-1 sp. Repeat from * to end. Join with a ss into top of beginning ch-3. Fasten off.

ROUND 5: Join Bleu Layette into first ch-3 sp, [ch 3 (counts as first dc), 3 dc, ch 3, 4 dc] into same sp, ch 1, skip next ch-1 sp, * (4 dc, ch 3, 4 dc) into next ch-3 sp, ch 1, skip next ch-1 sp. Repeat from * to end. Join with a ss into top of beginning ch-3. Fasten off.

ROUND 6: Join Rose Layette into first ch-3 sp, [ch 3 (counts as first dc), 4 dc, ch 3, 5 dc] into same sp, ch 1, skip next ch-1 sp, * (5 dc, ch 3, 5 dc) into next ch-3 sp , ch 1, skip next ch-1 sp. Repeat from * to end. Join with a ss into top of beginning ch-3. Fasten off.

ROUND 7: Join Blé into first ch-3 sp, ch 3 (counts as first dc), 9 dc into same sp, 1 sc into next ch-1 sp, * 10 dc into next ch-3 sp, 1 sc in next ch 1 sp. Repeat from * to end. Join with a ss into top of beginning ch-3. Fasten off.

14

African Flower Potholder

Materials

Hook: 3.5 mm
DMC Natura Just Cotton: 50g-115m
Colors:

	N 83	Blé
	N 06	Rose Layette
	N 32	Rose Soraya
	N 31	Malva
	N 12	Light Green
	N 05	Bleu Layette
	N 25	Aguamarina
	N 47	Safran
	N 23	Passion
	N 37	Canelle
	N 76	Bamboo
	N 30	Glicine
	N 64	Prussian

Finished size: 20 cm

Base Round: Ch 4, join with a ss into first ch to make a ring.

ROUND 1: Working into ring ch 3 (counts as first dc), 1 dc, ch 1, * 2 dc, ch 1. Repeat from * 6 more times. Join with a ss into top of beginning ch-3. Fasten off. (8 sets of 2dc and 8 ch-1 sps)

ROUND 2: Join new color into first ch-1 sp, [ch 3 (counts as first dc), 1 dc, ch 2, 2 dc] into same sp, ch 1. *(2 dc, ch 2, 2 dc) into next sp, ch 1. Repeat from * to end. Join with a ss into top of beginning ch-3.

ROUND 3: ss into first ch-2 sp from previous round, [ch 3 (counts as first dc), 6 dc] into same sp, ch 1, * 7 dc into next ch-2 sp, ch 1. Repeat from * to end. Join with a ss into top of beginning ch-3. Fasten off.

ROUND 4: Join new color into top of first dc of previous round, ch 1, sc into same st, sc into the top of the next 6 dc of previous round,

*make a long sc down into Round 1 between dc sts, sc into next 7 dc. Repeat from * 6 more times, make a long sc. Join with a ss into top of beginning ch-1. Fasten off.

ROUND 5: Join new color into first sc of previous round, ch 1, sc into same sp, sc into each st to end. Join with a ss into top of beginning ch-1. Fasten off. (64 sc)

ROUND 6: Join new color into center st of first petal, ch 4 (counts as first dc and ch 1), dc into same st, * dc into next 7 sts, * (1 dc, ch 1, 1 dc) into next st (top of flower petal), dc into next 7 sts. Repeat from * to end. Join with a ss into top of beginning ch-3. Fasten off

ROUND 7: Join new color into first ch-1 sp, [ch 2 (counts as first sc and ch 1), 1 sc] into same sp, sc into next 9 sts,* (1 sc, ch 1, 1 sc) into ch-1 sp, sc into next 9 sts. Repeat from * to end. Join with a ss into top of beginning ch-1. Fasten off.

ROUND 8: Join new color into first ch-1 sp, [ch 4 (counts as first dc and ch 1), 1 dc] into same sp, dc into next 11 sts, * (1 dc, ch 1, 1 dc) into ch-1 sp, dc into next 11 sts. Repeat from * to end. Join with a ss into top of beginning ch-3. Fasten off.

ROUND 9: Join new color into first ch-1 sp, ch 2 [counts as first sc and ch 1), 1 sc] into same sp, sc into next 13 sts, * (1 sc, ch 1, 1 sc) into ch-1 sp, sc into next 13 sts. Repeat from * to end. Join with a ss into top of beginning ch-1. Fasten off.

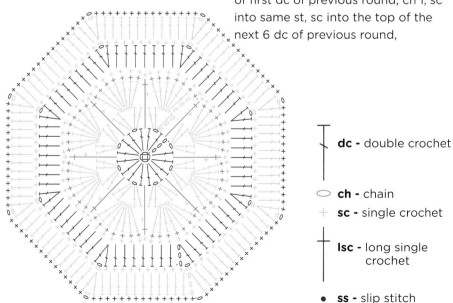

dc -	double crochet
ch -	chain
sc -	single crochet
lsc -	long single crochet
ss -	slip stitch

Blue Flower Potholder

Materials

Hook: 3.5 mm
DMC Natura Just Cotton: 50g-115m
Colors:

- N 05 Bleu Layette
- N 02 Ivory
- N 25 Aguamarina
- N 23 Passion
- N 06 Rose Layette

Popcorn st: 4 dc into same st, remove hook and insert through top of first dc, pull loop through.

Note: The first popcorn st in a round is started differently to subsequent popcorn sts in round. Instructions for the first popcorn are included within the pattern. For subsequent popcorns follow the instructions above.

Puff st: Yo, insert hook into st, yo, draw loop up to desired stitch height (3 loops) on hook. Repeat 3 more times into same st, yo, draw through all 9 loops on hook. Ch 1 to secure.

Finished size: 21 x 21 cm

Base Round: Using Ivory, ch 4, join with a ss into first ch to make a ring.
ROUND 1: Working into ring, ch 1 (not counted as a st), 8 sc. Join with a ss into top of first sc.
ROUND 2: Ch 3 (counts as first dc), 3 dc into same st, remove hook from loop and insert through top of beginning ch-3, pull loop through (first popcorn st made), ch 2, * make popcorn st in next st, ch 2. Repeat from * 6 more times. Join with a ss into top of first popcorn. Fasten off. (8 popcorn sts)
ROUND 3: Join Bleu Layette into first ch-2 sp, make * (puff st, ch 5, puff st) into same sp, ch 5, 1 sc into next ch sp, ch 5. Repeat from * to end. Join with a ss into top of first puff st. Fasten off.

Blue flower motif – Make 3

Note: These motifs are joined-as-you-go in Round 3. Motif layout is 2 across and 2 down.
Base Round: Using Bleu Layette, ch 4, join with a ss into first ch to make a ring.
ROUND 1: Working into ring, ch 1 (not counted as a st), sc 8. Join with a ss into top of beginning sc.
ROUND 2: Ch 3 (counts as first dc), 3 dc into same st, remove hook from loop and insert through top of beginning ch-3, pull loop through (first popcorn st made), ch 2, * make popcorn st in next st, ch 2. Repeat from * 6 more times. Join with a ss into top of popcorn. (8 popcorn sts).

 Puff stitch

 First popcorn

+	**sc -** single crochet
⊙	**ch -** chain
•	**ss -** slip stitch
	pc - popcorn

ROUND 3: ss into first ch-2 sp, make a puff st, ch 2, begin joining new motif to previous motif, insert hook into 3rd ch in a corner ch-5 on previous motif, yo and make a sc, ch 2, make another puff st into new motif in same sp, ch 2, insert hook into 3rd ch of next ch-5 on previous motif, yo and make a sc, ch 2, 1 sc into next ch-2 sp on new motif, ch 2, insert hook into 3rd ch of next ch-5 on previous motif, yo and make a sc, ch 2, make a puff st in next ch-2 sp on new motif, ch 2, insert hook into 3rd ch in corner ch-5 on previous motif, yo and make a sc, ch 2, make another puff st into same sp on new motif. Remainder of round is worked into new motif only, ch 5, sc into next ch-2 sp, ch 5, * (puff st, ch 5, puff st) into next ch-5 sp, ch 5, sc into next ch-2 sp, ch 5. Repeat from * to end. Join with a ss into top of first puff st. Fasten off

Continue joining remaining 2 motifs this way.

Border

ROUND 1: Rejoin yarn into first corner ch-5 sp, [ch 2 (counts as first hdc), 7 hdc] into same sp (corner made), 4 hdc into next 6 ch-5 sps, *8 hdc into next ch-5 sp, 4 hdc into next 6 ch-5 sps. Repeat from * to end. Join with a ss into top of beginning ch-2. Fasten off.

ROUND 2: Join Passion into a corner between 4th and 5th sts of previous round, ch 2 (counts as first sc and ch 1), 1 sc into same sp, sc into each st up to next corner, *(1 sc, ch 1, 1 sc) between 4th and 5th sts in corner, sc into each st up to next corner. Repeat from * to end. Join with a ss into top of beginning ch-1. Fasten off.

ROUND 3: Join Ivory into corner ch-1 sp, [ch 2 (counts as first sc and ch 1], 1 sc into same sp, sc into each st up to next corner sp, *(1 sc, ch 1, 1 sc) into sp, sc into each st up to next corner. Repeat from * to end. Join with a ss into top of beginning ch-1. Fasten off.

ROUND 4: Join Aguamarina into corner ch-1 sp, [ch 2 (counts as first sc and ch 1], 1 sc into same sp, sc into each st up to next corner sp, *(1 sc, ch 1, 1 sc) into sp, sc into each st up to next corner. Repeat from * to end. Join with a ss into top of beginning ch-1. Fasten off.

Finished Size
21 x 21 cm

Apron

Materials

Fabric for apron
Hook: 3.5 mm
Fabric button
DMC Natura Just Cotton: 50g-115m
Colors:

- N 02 Ivory
- N 25 Aguamarina
- N 23 Passion

Finished size: 50 x 65 cm

Pocket size: 13 x 13 cm

Apron fabric size: 50 x 70 cm

Tie size: 265 x 7 cm

Stitch hem along 3 edges of apron. Fold top of apron down 3 cm and stitch to apron tie.

Pocket

Foundation row: Using Ivory, ch 23
ROW 1: sc into 2nd ch from hook, sc 21. Ch 1, turn.
ROW 2: sc 22. Ch 1, turn.
ROWS 3 – 27: Repeat Row 2, changing color for Passion in Rows 7, 14 and 21. Fasten off.

Pocket Border

Join Aguamarina into top right hand corner of pocket, ch 1 (counts as first sc), sc into next 5 sts, (1 sc, ch 3, 1 sc) into next st, sc into next 4 sts, (1 sc, ch 3, 1 sc) into next st, sc into next 4 sts, (1 sc, ch 3, 1 sc) into next st, sc into next 5 sts. Sc around remaining edges.
Join with a ss into top of beginning ch-1. Fasten off.
Sew pocket to apron.

Apron Hem Border

Using Ivory, sew evenly spaced blanket stitches along bottom edge of apron. Fasten off.
ROW 1: With right side facing, join yarn into first sp between stitches, sc 2 into each sp to end. Ch 1, turn.
ROW 2: sc into each st to end. Ch 1, turn.
ROW 3: sc into each st to end. Turn. Fasten off.
ROW 4: Join Passion, ch 1 (not counted as a st), sc into same st, sc into each st to end. Turn. Fasten off.
ROW 5: Join Ivory, ch 1 (not counted as a st), sc into same st, sc into each st to end. Ch 1, turn.
ROW 6: sc in each sc sc into each st to end. Ch 1, turn.
ROW 7: Sc into first st, * skip 2 sts, 5 hdc into next st, skip 2 sts, 1 sc into next st. Repeat from * to end. Fasten off.

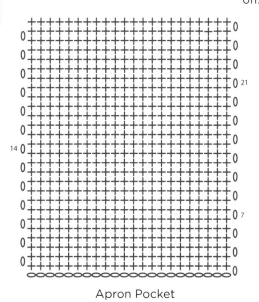

Apron Pocket

Hem Border Trim

○ **ch -** chain

+ **sc -** single crochet

| **hdc -** half double crochet

23

African Flower Garland

Materials

Hook: 3.5 mm
DMC Natura Just Cotton: 50g-115m
Colors:

	N 83	Blé
	N 81	Acanthe
	N 06	Rose Layette
	N 32	Rose Soraya
	N 30	Glicine
	N 31	Malva
	N 12	Light Green
	N 76	Bamboo
	N 05	Bleu Layette
	N 25	Aguamarina
	N 02	Ivory

Finished size: Length: 137 cm

For African Flower

Use same chart as **African Flower Potholder** page 15 only up to (and including) Round 4.

	hdc - half double crochet
	dc - double crochet
	ch - chain
	sc - single crochet
	ss - slip stitch

African flower – Make 4

Base Round: Ch 4, join with a ss into first ch to make a ring.
ROUND 1: Working into ring ch 3 (counts as first dc), 1 dc, ch 1, * 2 dc, ch 1. Repeat from * 6 more times. Join with a ss into top of beginning ch-3. Fasten off. (8 sets of 2dc and 8 ch-1 sps).
ROUND 2: Join new color into first ch-1 sp, [ch 3 (counts as first dc), 1 dc, ch 2, 2 dc] into same sp, ch 1. *(2 dc, ch 2, 2 dc) into next sp, ch 1. Repeat from * to end. Join with a ss into top of beginning ch-3.
ROUND 3: ss into first ch-2 sp from previous round, [ch 3 (counts as first dc), 6 dc] into same sp, ch 1, * 7 dc into next ch-2 sp, ch 1. Repeat from * to end. Join with a ss into top of beginning ch-3. Fasten off.
ROUND 4: Join new color into top of first dc of previous round, ch 1, sc into same st, sc into the top of the next 6 dc of previous round, * make a long sc down into Round 1 between dc sts, sc into next 7 dc. Repeat from * 6 more times, make a long sc. Join with a ss into top of beginning ch-1. Fasten off.

Small flower – Make 4

Base Round: Ch 4, join with a ss into first ch to make a ring.
ROUND 1: Working into ring, ch 4 (counts as first hdc and ch 2), * 1 hdc, ch 2. Repeat from * 4 more times. Join with a ss into 2nd ch of beginning ch-4 (6 hdc/6 ch-2 sps)
ROUND 2: Ss into first ch-2 sp, * (1 sc, 5 dc, 1 sc) into same sp. Repeat from * into each ch sp to end. Join with a ss into top of first sc. Fasten off.
ROUND 3: Join new color into first st of previous round, ch 1 (not counted as a st), sc into same st, sc into each st to end. Join with a ss into top of beginning ch-1. Fasten off.

Joining

Using Ivory, ch 50, join to top of Small Flower petal with a sc, ch 15, join to top of African Flower petal with a sc. Continue joining flowers this way to end, ch 50. Fasten off.

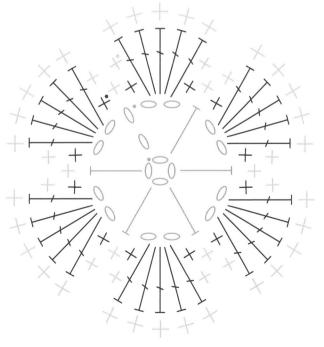

Small Flower

Bag

Materials

Hook: 5 mm
DMC Natura Just Cotton: 50g-115m
Colors:

- N 01   Ibiza
- N 45   Orquidea
- N 33   Amaranto
- N 47   Safran
- N 83   Blé
- N 81   Acanthe

Finished size: 28 x 32 cm

Star Stitch Instructions

Beginning Star Stitch: Ch 3, insert hook into 2nd ch from hook, yo, pull up loop, insert hook into 3rd ch from hook, yo, pull up loop, insert hook into 1st sc of previous row, yo, pull up loop, repeat into next 2 sts (6 loops on hook), yo, pull through all loops on hook, ch 1 to secure stitch.

Star Stitch: Insert hook through the eye formed by the ch-1 in previous st, yo, pull up loop, insert hook under the last spike in the previous star made, yo, pull up loop, insert hook into the same st that the previous star was made, yo, pull up loop, repeat into next 2 sts (6 loops on hook), yo pull through all loops on hook, ch 1 to secure stitch.

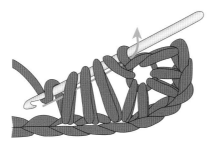

Star Stitch

Note: This pattern uses 2 strands of yarn held together.

Back

Foundation Row: Using Ibiza and Amaranto, ch 45.

ROW 1: Insert hook into 2nd ch from hook, yo, pull up loop, repeat the same into the 3rd, 4th, 5th and 6th chains from hook (6 loops on hook), yo, draw through all 6 loops on hook, ch 1 to close st (first star made). Insert hook through the eye formed by the ch-1, yo, pull up loop, insert hook under the last spike in the first star made, yo, pull up loop, insert hook into the same ch that the previous star was made, yo, pull up loop, repeat into next 2 ch, yo pull through all 6 loops on hook, ch 1 (second star made). Continue making stars this way to last ch, 1 hdc in last ch. Turn.

ROW 2: Ch 1, 1 sc into hdc of previous row, 1 sc into the eye of first star, 2 sc into each eye across to last st, sc into top of ch in previous row. Turn.

ROW 3: Make a Beginning Star St into first st, star st into each stitch to last st, 1 hdc in last st. Turn

ROW 4: Ch 1, 1 sc into hdc of previous row, 1 sc into the eye of first star, 2 sc into each eye across to last st, sc into top of ch in previous row. Turn.

ROWS 5 – 30: Repeat Rows 3 and 4. Fasten off after last row.

Front

Foundation Row: Using Ibiza and Orquidea, ch 45.

ROWS 1 – 18: Work the same as for Front. Fasten off.

ROWS 19 – 30: Change colors for Acanthe and Orquidea and continue working in pattern. Fasten off after last row.

Finishing

Lay the front and back pieces on top of each other, with right sides facing up. Using Acanthe and Safran, sc both pieces together down one side, work 2 sc into corner, continue joining with sc along bottom, 2 sc into next corner, sc up remaining side, ch 120 for strap. Join with a ss into first sc. Turn, ch 1, sc into each ch of bag strap. Join with a ss into sc on the top corner of bag.

Flower Brooch

Foundation row: Using Acanthe, ch 81.

ROW 1: sc into 2nd ch from hook, * ch 2, skip next ch, sc into next ch. Repeat from * to end. Turn.

ROW 2: * (ss, ch 1, 3 hdc, ch 1, ss) in ch-2 sp. Repeat from * into next 14 ch-2 sps. Fasten off Acanthe and join in Blé, continue working from * into the next 15 ch-2 sps. Fasten off.

Finishing

Roll up into flower shape. Use a yarn needle to stitch flower together at the back. Stitch ribbon pieces to the back of the flower and attach a safety pin.

hdc - half double crochet

ch - chain

sc - single crochet

ss - slip stitch

Purse

Materials

Hook: 3.5 mm
DMC Natura Just Cotton: 50g-115 mm
Colors:

- N 64 Prussian
- N 47 Safran
- N 23 Passion
- N 01 Ibiza

Joining color:

- N 83 Blé

Popcorn st: 4 dc into same st, remove hook and insert through top of first dc, pull loop through.

Note: The first popcorn st in a round is started differently to subsequent popcorn sts in round. Instructions for the first popcorn are included within the pattern. For subsequent popcorns follow the instructions above.

4-Bobble st: yo and insert hook into st, yo, draw loop through, yo, draw through first 2 loops on hook. Repeat 3 more times into same st (5 loops on hook), yo and draw through all loops on hook.

Note: The first bobble st in a round is started differently to subsequent bobbles in round. Instructions for the first bobble are included within the pattern. For subsequent bobbles follow the instructions above.

Finished size: Square: 11 x 11 cm

Make 2 in the following colour sequences:

1. Rnd 1 – Prussian / Rnds 2 & 3 – Ibiza / Rnd 4 – Passion / Rnd 5 – Safran

2. Rnd 1 – Passion / Rnds 2 & 3 – Ibiza / Rnd 4 – Prussian / Rnd 5 – Safran

Base Round: Using Prussian or Passion, ch 4, ss into first ch to form a ring.

ROUND 1: Ch 5 (counts as first dc and ch-2), *1 dc, ch 2. Repeat from * 6 more times. Join with a ss into top of 3rd ch in starting ch. Fasten off. (8 dc and 8 ch-2 sps)

ROUND 2: Join Ibiza into first ch-2 sp of previous round, ch 3 (counts as first dc), 3 dc into same sp, remove hook from loop and insert through top of beginning ch-3, pull loop through (first popcorn st made), ch 2, * make popcorn st in next sp, ch 2. Repeat from * to end. Join with a ss into top of first popcorn st. (8 popcorn sts).

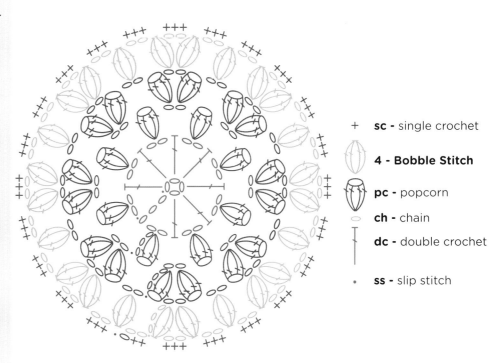

+	**sc -** single crochet
	4 - Bobble Stitch
	pc - popcorn
	ch - chain
	dc - double crochet
•	**ss -** slip stitch

ROUND 3: ss over to next ch-2 sp of previous round, ch 3 (counts as first dc), 3 dc into same sp, remove hook from loop and insert through top of beginning ch-3, pull loop through (first popcorn st made), ch 2, make another popcorn st into same sp, ch 2, *(popcorn st, ch 2, popcorn st) into next ch-2 sp, ch 2. Repeat from * to end. Join with a ss into top of first popcorn st. Fasten off. (16 popcorn sts).

ROUND 4: Join Prussian or Passion into first ch-2 sp of previous round, ch 3 (counts as first dc), yo and insert hook into same sp, yo, draw loop through, yo, draw through first 2 loops on hook. Repeat 2 more times into same sp (4 loops on hook), yo and draw through all loops on hook (first 4-bobble made), ch 2, make another bobble st into same sp, ch 2, 4 bobble st into next sp, ch 2, *(4-bobble st, ch 2, 4-bobble st) into next sp, ch 2, 4-bobble st into next sp, ch 2. Repeat from * to end. Join with a ss into top of beginning ch-3. Fasten off. (24 4-bobble sts)

ROUND 5: Join Safran into first ch-2 sp of previous round, ch 1 (counts as first sc), 2 sc into same sp, 3 sc into each ch-2 sp to end. Join with a ss into beginning ch-1. Fasten off.

Finishing

Stitch the tops of both motifs to clasp. Using Blé, sc both motifs together. Fasten off.

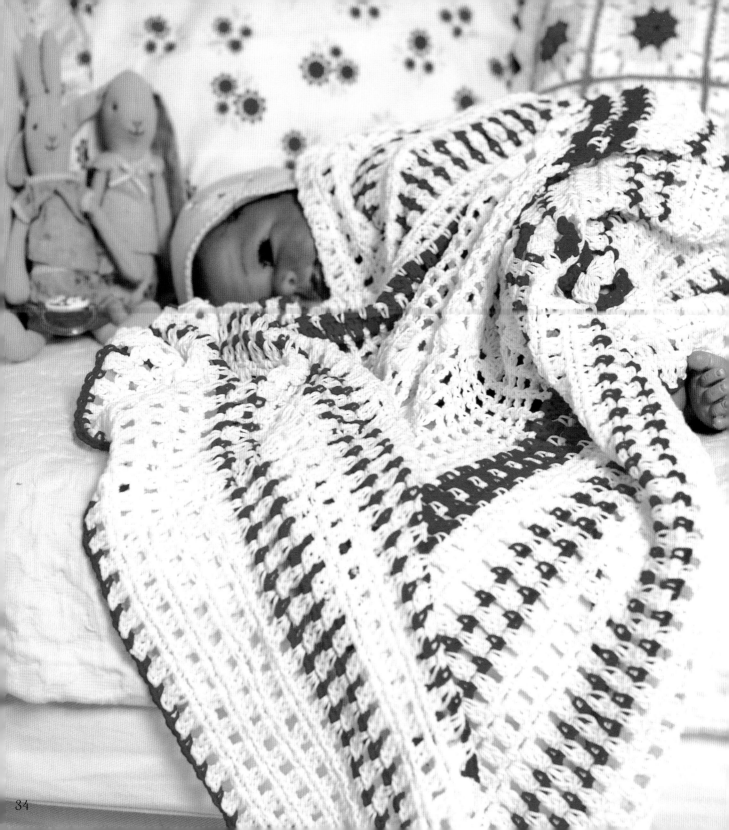

Baby Blanket

Materials

Hook: 3.5 mm
DMC Natura Just Cotton: 50g-115m
Colors:

- ○ N 01 Ibiza -4 balls
- ● N 23 Passion -1 ball

Finished size: 80 cm X 80 cm

○ **ch -** chain

| **dc -** double crochet

● **ss -** slip stitch

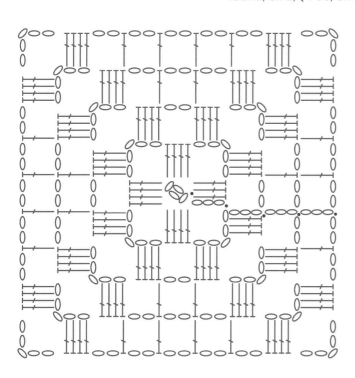

Base round: Using Ibiza, ch 4, join with a ss into first ch to make a ring.
ROUND 1: Working into ring, ch 3 (counts as first dc), 3 dc, ch 5, *4 dc, ch 5. Repeat from * twice more. Join with a ss into top of beginning ch-3. Turn.
ROUND 2: Ch 3 (counts as first dc), (ch 5, 4 dc) into same sp, ch 2, * (4 dc, ch 5, 4 dc) into next sp, ch 2. Repeat from * to end. Join with a ss into top of beginning ch-3. Turn.
ROUND 3: Ch 5 (counts as dc and ch 2), * dc into first dc of cluster in previous round, ch 2, (4 dc, ch 5, 4 dc) into next ch-5 sp, ch 2, dc into 4th dc of cluster in previous round, ch 2. Repeat from * twice more, dc into first dc of cluster in previous round, ch 2, (4 dc, ch 5, 4 dc) into

next ch-5 sp, ch 2. Join with a ss into top of 3rd ch of beginning ch. Turn.
ROUND 4: Ch 5 (counts as dc and ch 2), * dc into next dc in previous round, ch 2, dc into first dc of cluster in previous round, ch 2, (4 dc, ch 5, 4 dc) into next ch-5 sp, ch 2, dc into 4th dc of cluster in previous round, ch 2, dc into next dc of previous round, ch 2. Repeat from * to end. Join with a ss into top of 3rd ch of beginning ch. Turn.
ROUNDS 5-11: Continue working this way, making (4 dc, ch 5, 4 dc) in each corner, 1 dc into top of each dc between corners and also into the first and last dc of each corner cluster. Join with a ss into top of beginning ch-3. Fasten off.
ROUND 12: Join Passion into first ch-2 sp of previous round, ch 3 (counts as first dc), 1 dc into same sp, ch 1, * 2 dc into next ch-2 sp, ch 1 **. Repeat from * to ** into each ch-2 sp and make (4 dc, ch 5, 4 dc) into each ch-5 corner space to end. Join with a ss into top of beginning ch-3. Fasten off.
ROUND 13: Join Ibiza into first ch-1 sp, ch 3 (counts as first sc and ch 2), * sc into next ch-1 sp, ch 2 **. Repeat from * to ** into each ch-1 sp and make (3 sc, ch 5, 3 sc) into each ch-5 corner space to end. Join with a ss into top of beginning ch-1. Fasten off.
ROUND 14: Join Passion into first ch-2 sp, ch 3 (counts as first dc), dc

into same sp, ch 1, * 2 dc into next ch-2 sp, ch 1 **. Repeat from * to ** into each ch-2 sp and make (4 dc, ch 5, 4 dc) into each ch-5 corner space to end. Join with a ss into top of beginning ch-1. Fasten off.

ROUND 15: Join Ibiza into first ch-1 sp, ch 3 (counts as first sc and ch 2), * sc into next ch-1 sp, ch 2 **. Repeat from * to ** into each ch-1 sp, and make (3 sc, ch 5, 3 sc) into each ch-5 corner space. Join with a ss into top of beginning ch-1. Do not turn.

ROUND 16: ss into ch sp, ch 3 (counts as first dc), dc into same space, ch 1, * 2 dc into next sp, ch 1 **. Repeat from * to ** into each ch-2 sp, and make (3 sc, ch 5, 3 sc) into each ch-5 corner space. Join with a ss into top of beginning ch-3. Do not turn.

ROUND 17: ss into ch sp, ch 3 (counts as first sc and ch 2), * sc into next ch-1 sp, ch 2 **. Repeat from * to ** into each ch-1 sp, and make (3 sc, ch 5, 3 sc) into each ch-5 corner space. Join with a ss into top of beginning ch-1. Do not turn

ROUND 18: ss into ch sp, ch 3 (counts as first dc), dc into same space, ch 1, * 2 dc into next sp, ch 1 **. Repeat from * to ** into each ch-2 sp, and make (3 sc, ch 5, 3 sc) into each ch-5 corner space. Join with a ss into top of beginning ch-3. Fasten off.

ROUND 19: Join Passion into first ch-1 sp, ch 3 (counts as first sc and ch 2), * sc into next ch-1 sp, ch 2 **. Repeat from * to ** into each ch-1 sp, and make (3 sc, ch 5, 3 sc) into each ch-5 corner space. Join with a ss into top of beginning ch-1. Fasten off.

ROUND 20: Join Ibiza into first ch-2 sp, ch 3 (counts as first dc), dc into same space, ch 1, * 2 dc into next sp, ch 1 **. Repeat from * to ** into each ch-2 sp, and make (3 sc, ch 5, 3 sc) into each ch-5 corner space. Join with a ss into top of beginning ch-3. Fasten off.

ROUND 21: Join Passion into first ch-1 sp, ch 3 (counts as first sc and ch 2), * sc into next ch-1 sp, ch 2 **. Repeat from * to ** into each ch-1 sp, and make (3 sc, ch 5, 3 sc) into each ch-5 corner space. Join with a ss into top of beginning ch-1. Fasten off.

ROUND 22: Join Ibiza into first ch-2 sp, ch 3 (counts as first dc), dc into same space, ch 1, * 2 dc into next sp, ch 1 **. Repeat from * to ** into each ch-2 sp, and make (3

sc, ch 5, 3 sc) into each ch-5 corner space. Join with a ss into top of beginning ch-3. Do not turn.

ROUND 23: ss into ch sp, ch 3 (counts as first sc and ch 2), * sc into next ch-1 sp, ch 2 **. Repeat from * to ** into each ch-1 sp, and make (3 sc, ch 5, 3 sc) into each ch-5 corner space. Join with a ss into top of beginning ch-1. Do not turn

ROUND 24: ss into ch sp, ch 3 (counts as first dc), dc into same space, ch 1, * 2 dc into next sp, ch 1 **. Repeat from * to ** into each ch-2 sp, and make (3 sc, ch 5, 3 sc) into each ch-5 corner space. Join with a ss into top of beginning ch-3. Do not turn.

ROUND 25: ss into ch sp, ch 3 (counts as first sc and ch 2), * sc into next ch-1 sp, ch 2 **. Repeat from * to ** into each ch-1 sp, and make (3 sc, ch 5, 3 sc) into each ch-5 corner space. Join with a ss into top of beginning ch-1. Do not turn.

ROUND 26: ss into ch sp, ch 3 (counts as first dc), dc into same space, ch 1, * 2 dc into next sp, ch 1 ** . Repeat from * to ** into each ch-2 sp, and make (3 sc, ch 5, 3 sc) into each ch-5 corner space. Join with a ss into top of beginning ch-3. Fasten off.

ROUND 27: Join Passion into first ch-1 sp, ch 3 (counts as first sc and ch 2), * sc into next ch-1 sp, ch 2 **. Repeat from * to ** into each ch-1 sp, and make (3 sc, ch 5, 3 sc) into each ch-5 corner space. Join with a ss into top of beginning ch-1. Fasten off.

ROUND 28: Join Ibiza into first ch-2 sp, ch 3 (counts as first dc), dc into same space, ch 1, * 2 dc into next sp, ch 1 **. Repeat from * to ** into each ch-2 sp, and make (3 sc, ch 5, 3 sc) into each ch-5 corner space. Join with a ss into top of beginning ch-3. Fasten off.

ROUND 29: Join Passion into first ch-1 sp, ch 3 (counts as first sc and ch 2), * sc into next ch-1 sp, ch 2 **. Repeat from * to ** into each ch-1 sp, and make (3 sc, ch 5, 3 sc) into each ch-5 corner space. Join with a ss into top of beginning ch-1. Fasten off.

ROUND 30: Join Ibiza into first ch-2 sp, ch 3 (counts as first dc), dc into same space, ch 1, * 2 dc into next sp, ch 1 **. Repeat from * to ** into each ch-2 sp, and make (3 sc, ch 5, 3 sc) into each ch-5 corner space. Join with a ss into top of beginning ch-3. Do not turn.

ROUNDS 31, 33, 35, 37: ss into ch sp, ch 3 (counts as first sc and ch 2), * sc into next ch-1 sp, ch 2 **. Repeat from * to ** into each ch-1 sp, and make (3 sc, ch 5, 3 sc) into each ch-5 corner space. Join with a ss into top of beginning ch-1. Do not turn.

ROUNDS 32, 34, 36, 38: ss into ch sp, ch 3 (counts as first dc), dc into same space, ch 1, * 2 dc into next sp, ch 1 ** . Repeat from * to ** into each ch-2 sp, and make (3 sc, ch 5, 3 sc) into each ch-5 corner space. Join with

a ss into top of beginning ch-3. Do not turn between rows. Fasten off after Row 38.

ROUND 39: Join Passion into first ch-1 sp, ch 3 (counts as first sc and ch 2), * sc into next ch-1 sp, ch 2 **. Repeat from * to ** into each ch-1 sp, and make (3 sc, ch 5, 3 sc) into each ch-5 corner space. Join with a ss into top of beginning ch-1. Fasten off.

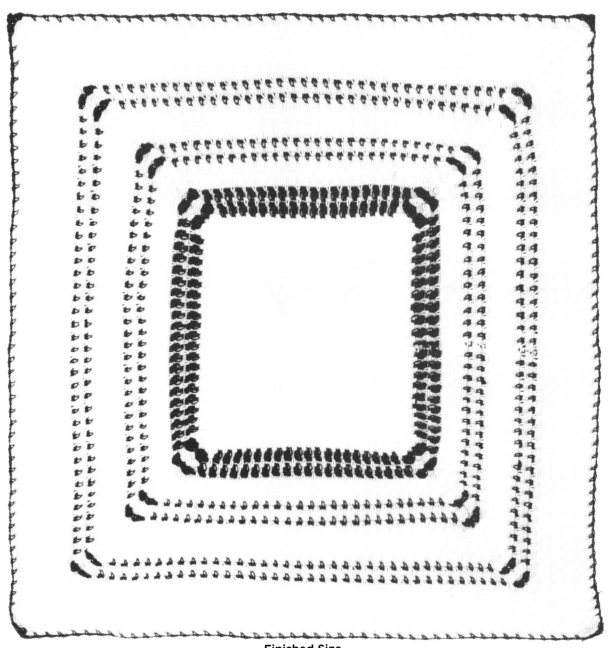

Finished Size
80 cm X 80 cm

Baby Booties

Materials

Hook: 3.5 mm
DMC Natura Just Cotton: 50g-115m
Colors:

N 06 Rose Layette

Fabric ribbon

hdc2tog: yo, insert hook into st, pull up a loop (3 loops on hook), yo, insert hook into next st, pull up loop (5 loops on hook), yo, pull through all 5 loops on hook.
Finished size: 9 cm length
To fit: 0-3 month

Foundation row: Ch 10

ROUND 1: In 3rd ch from hook, 2 hdc into same ch, hdc into next 6 ch, 6 hdc into last ch. Flip your work around and working into the bottom of your foundation ch sts, hdc into next 6 ch, 3 hdc into last ch. Join with a ss into top of beginning ch.
ROUND 2: Ch 3 (counts as first dc), 1 dc into same st, 2 dc into next 2 sts, 1 dc into next 5 sts, 2 dc into next 6 sts, 1 dc into next 5 sts, 2 dc into next 3 sts. Join with a ss into top of beginning ch-3.

ROUND 3: Stitches in this round are worked into the back loop only.
Ch 2 (counts as first hdc), hdc into each st to end. Join with a ss into top of beginning ch-2.
ROUND 4: Ch 2 (counts as first hdc), hdc into next 8 sts, hdc2tog 8 times, hdc into next 9 sts. Join with a ss into top of beginning ch-2.
ROUND 5: Ch 2 (counts as first hdc), hdc into ea st to end. Join with a ss into top of beginning ch-2.
Ribbon loop: Ch 5, ss to first ch. Fasten off.
Finishing: Tie ribbon into ribbon loop.

Finished Size
9 cm length

Kids Slippers

Materials

Hook: 3.5 mm
DMC Natura Just Cotton: 50g-115m
Colors:

- N 02 Ivory
- N 06 Rose Layette

Fabric ribbon
Finished size: 19 cm length
Slippers are made with 2 strands of yarn held together.

Note: This pattern uses 2 strands of yarn held together.
Base Round: Using Ivory, ch 4, join with a ss into first ch to make a ring.
ROUND 1: Working into ring, ch 1 (does not count as first st), 8 sc. Join with a ss into top of beginning ch-1. Fasten off. (8 sc)
ROUND 2: Join Rose Layette, ch 3 (counts as first dc), dc into same st, 2 dc into each st to end. Join with a ss into top of beginning ch 3. (16 dc)
ROUND 3: ch 3 (counts as first dc), 2 dc into next st, * 1 dc into next st, 2 dc into next st. Repeat from * to end. Join with a ss into top of beginning ch-3. (24 dc)

ROUNDS 4 - 7: ch 3 (counts as first dc), dc into each st to end. Join with a ss into top of beginning ch-3. (24 dc)
ROWS 8 - 13: ch 3 (counts as first dc), dc into next 19 sts. Turn. (20 dc). Fasten off after last row completed.
ROW 14: Join Ivory, ch 3 (counts as first dc), dc into next 19 sts. Turn. (20 dc)
ROW 15: ch 1 (counts as first sc), sc into next 19 sts. Fasten off. (20 sc)

Finishing

Fold slipper right sides together, sew heel seam together. Thread ribbon through holes around top of slipper.

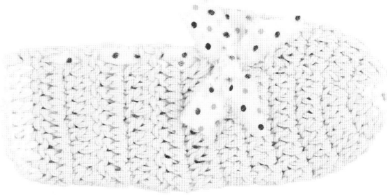

Finished Size
19 cm lenght

Bag

Materials

Hook: 3.5 mm
DMC Natura Just Cotton: 50g-115m
Colors:

- N 25 Aguamarina
- N 32 Rose Soraya
- N 12 Light Green
- N 02 Ivory

5-Bobble st: yo and insert hook into st, yo, draw loop through, yo, draw through first 2 loops on hook. Repeat 4 more times into same st (6 loops on hook), yo and draw through all loops on hook.

Note: The first bobble st in a round is started differently to subsequent bobbles in round. Instructions for the first bobble are included within the pattern. For subsequent bobbles follow the instructions above.

Finished size: 34 x 48 cm
5 squares across and 6 squares down

Square: 6 cm

Base Round: Using Light Green, ch 4, join with a ss into first ch to make a ring.

ROUND 1: Working into ring ch 5 (counts as first dc and ch 2), * 1 dc, ch 2, repeat from * 6 more times. Join with a ss into top of beginning ch-3. Fasten off. (8 dc, 8 x ch-2 sps). Make 60.

ROUND 2: Join Rose Soraya or Ivory into first ch 2 sp, ch 3 (counts as first dc), yo, insert hook into same sp, yo, draw up loop, yo, draw through first 2 loops on hook, repeat 3 more times into same sp (5 loops on hook), yo, draw through all 5 loops on hook (first 5-bobble stitch made), ch 2, 5-bobble stitch in next ch sp, ch 2. Repeat to end. Join with ss into top of first 5-bobble stitch. Fasten off. Make 30 using Rose Soraya and 30 using Ivory

ROUND 3: Join Aguamarina, into first ch-2 sp, ch 2 (counts as first hdc), 2 hdc into same sp, ch 1, (1 hdc, 2 dc, ch 3, 2 dc, 1 hdc) into next sp (corner made), ch 1, * 3 hdc into next sp, ch 1, (1 hdc, 2 dc, ch 3, 2 dc, 1 hdc) into next sp, ch 1. Repeat from * to end. Join with a ss into top of beginning ch-2. Fasten off

Join Motifs

Front and Back: Each 5 squares across and 6 squares down.
Lay motifs out with the squares laying side by side and right sides up. Beginning with the first 2 squares and starting with the square to your left, insert your hook through the back loop only of the first st, then insert hook into back loop of the first st in the next square, make a sc. Repeat to end. Continue joining the remaining squares this way. When all your squares have been joined across, join each strip of squares together in the same way. Fasten off.

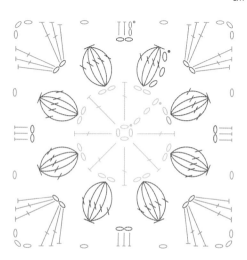

5 - Bobble stitch

ch - chain

sc - single crochet

hdc - half double crochet

ss - slip stitch

Finishing

ROW 1: Join yarn into top of front section, hdc into each st to end. Turn.

ROWS 2 – 9: ch 2 (counts as first hdc), hdc into each st to end. Fasten off after last row. Repeat for back section.

Fold strip of hdc crochet over bag handle and stitch together. Repeat for other handle.

Join bag sides together using the same method as squares were joined.

Stitch fabric lining inside bag.

Optional – decorate with a fabric flower and ribbons

Finished Size
34 x 48 cm

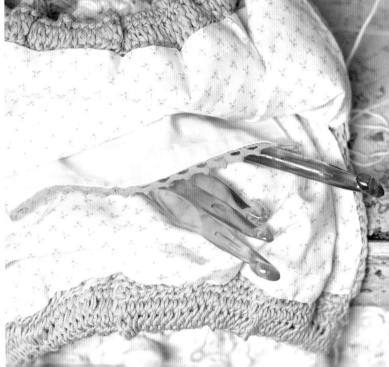

Sunburst Granny Baby Blanket

Materials

Hook: 3.5 mm
DMC Natura Just Cotton: 50g-115m
Colors:

- N 01 Ibiza- 7 balls
- N 25 Aguamarina- 1 ball
- N 23 Passion- 1 ball
- N 32 Rose Soraya- 1 ball
- N 06 Rose Layette- 1 ball
- N 10 Coral- 1 ball

Finished size: 110 x 120 cm
Total: 42 squares
Square: 14 cm

Make 42 squares in total using the following color combinations:

Make 14: Rnd 1 - Ibiza/Rnd 2 - Rose Soraya/Rnd 3 - Passion/Rnds 4-6 - Ibiza

Make 7: Rnd 1 - Ibiza/Rnd 2 - Rose Layette/Rnd 3 - Rose Soraya/Rnds 4-6 - Ibiza

Make 7: Rnd 1 - Ibiza/Rnd 2 - Rose Layette/Rnd 3 - Coral/Rnds 4-6: Ibiza

Make 4: Rnd 1- Passion/Rnds 2-6 – Ibiza

Make 3: Rnd 1 – Aguamarina/Rnds 2-6 – Ibiza

Make 7: Rnds 1-2 – Ibiza/Rnd 3 – Aguamarina/Rnds 4-6 - Ibiza

Base round: Ch 4, join with a ss into first ch to make a ring.

ROUND 1: Working into ring, ch 3 (counts as first dc), 11 dc. Join with a ss into top of beginning ch-3. Fasten off. (12 dc)

ROUND 2: Join new color into first sp between dc sts in previous round, ch 3 (counts as first dc), dc into same sp, ch 1, * 2 dc into next sp between dc sts in previous round, ch 1. Repeat from * to end. Join with a ss into top of beginning ch-3. Fasten off.

ROUND 3: Join new color into first ch-1 sp in previous round, ch 3 (counts as first dc), 2 dc into same sp, ch 1, * 3 dc into next sp, ch 1. Repeat from * to end. Join with a ss into top of beginning ch-3. Fasten off.

ROUND 4: Join new color into first ch-1 in previous round, ch 3 (counts as first dc, 2 dc into same sp, ch 1, 3 dc into next sp, ch 1, (3 dc, ch 2, 3 dc) into next sp (corner made), ch 1, * 3 dc into next sp, ch 1, 3 dc into next sp, ch 1, (3 dc, ch 2, 3 dc), ch 1. Repeat from * to end. Join with a ss into top of beginning ch-3. Do not turn.

ROUND 5: ss into next ch sp, ch 3 (counts as first dc), 2 dc into same sp, ch 1, 3 dc into next sp, ch 1, (3 dc, ch 2, 3 dc) into next sp (corner made), ch 1, * 3 dc, ch 1 into next 3 spaces, (3 dc, ch 2, 3 dc), ch 1. Repeat from * twice more, 3 dc into next sp, ch 1. Join with a ss into top of beginning ch-3. Do not turn.

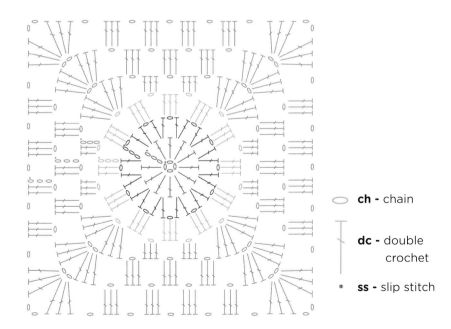

- **ch -** chain
- **dc -** double crochet
- **ss -** slip stitch

ROUND 6: ss into next ch sp, ch 3 (counts as first dc), 2 dc into same sp, ch 1, 3 dc into next sp, ch 1, (3 dc, ch 2, 3 dc) into next sp (corner made), ch 1, * 3 dc, ch 1 into next 4 spaces, (3 dc, ch 2, 3 dc), ch 1. Repeat from * twice more, 3 dc, ch 1 into next 2 spaces. Join with a ss into top of beginning ch-3. Fasten off.

Join motifs

6 squares across and 7 squares down

Use Rose Layette to join. Lay motifs out side by side and right sides up. Beginning with the first 2 squares and starting with the square to your left, insert your hook through the back loop only of the first st, then insert hook into back loop of the first st in the next square, make a sc. Repeat to end. Continue joining the remaining squares this way. When all your squares have been joined across, join each strip of squares together in the same way. Fasten off.

Border
ROUND 1: Using Rose Layette, sc through the back loop only into each around joined motifs, working (1 sc, ch 1, 1 sc) into each corner sp. Fasten off.
ROUND 2: Join Passion and work the same as for Round 1. Fasten off.
ROUND 3: Join Rose Layette, hdc into each st around, working (1 hdc, ch 1, 1 hdc) into each corner sp.
ROUND 4: Continuing with Rose Layette, work the same as for Round 3. Fasten off.
ROUND 5: Join Aguamarina and work the same as for Round 3. Fasten off.
ROUND 6: Join Rose Layette, sc into each st around, working (1 sc, ch 1, 1 sc) into each corner sp. Fasten off.

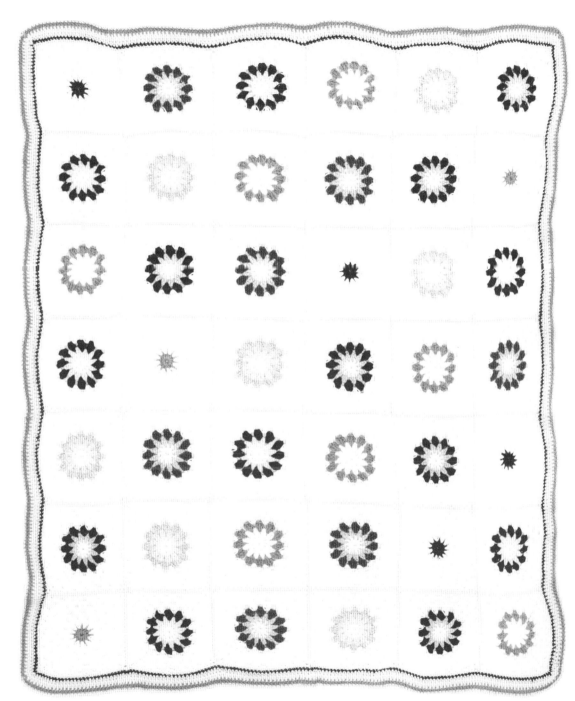

Finished Size
110 x 120 cm

Baby Dress

Materials

Hook: 3.5 mm
DMC Natura Just Cotton: 50g-115m
Colors:

- N 01   Ibiza
- N 23   Passion

Ribbon
Finished size: 44 cm around the chest/34 cm length
To fit : 0-3 months

Foundation chain: Using Ibiza, Ch 80. Join with a ss to first ch to make a ring.

Note: Join will be centre back

ROUND 1: Ch 1 (counts as first sc), sc into each ch. Join with a ss into top of beginning ch-1.
(80 sc)

ROUND 2: Work as for Round 1. Fasten off.

ROUND 3: Join Passion. Work as for Round 1. Fasten off.

ROUNDS 4 - 5: Join Ibiza, Work as for Round 1.

ROUND 6: Ch 3 (counts as first dc), dc into next 9 sts, ch 20 (first arm-hole), skip next 20 sts, dc into next 20 sts, ch 20 (second armhole), skip next 20 sts, dc into next 10 sts. Join with a ss into beginning ch-3.

ROUND 7: ch 3 (counts as first dc), dc into each st (including each arm-hole ch) to end. Join with a ss into beginning ch-3.

ROUNDS 8 – 10: ch 3 (counts as first dc), dc into each st to end. Join with a ss into beginning ch-3. Fasten off after last round.

ROUND 11: Join Passion, ch 3 (counts as first dc), dc into same st, skip next st, * 2 dc into next st, skip next st. Repeat from * to end. Join with a ss into top of beginning ch-3.

ROUNDS 12-29: ss into space be-tween first 2-dc in previous round, ch 3 (counts as first dc), dc into same sp, * 2 dc between each 2 dc in previous round. Repeat from * to end. Join with a ss into top of beginning ch-3. Fasten off after last round.

Finishing: Thread ribbon between stitches in Round 10.

Finished Size
44 cm around the chest/34 cm length

Pastel Pillow

Materials

Hook: 3.5 mm
DMC Natura Just Cotton: 50g-115m
Colors:

- N 12 Light Green
- N 32 Rose Soraya
- N 81 Acanthe
- N 02 Ivory
- N 25 Aguamarina
- N 30 Glicine

Puff stitch: yo, insert hook into st, yo, draw loop up to desired stitch height (3 loops) on hook. Repeat 3 more times into same st, yo, draw through all 9 loops on hook. Ch 1 to secure.
Finished size: 42 x 42 cm

Puff Stitch motif - pillow front

Make 25 squares in total: 13 squares with Acanthe in the center and 12 squares with Rose Soraya

Base Round: Using Rose Soraya or Acanthe ch 4, join with a ss into first ch to make a ring.
ROUND 1: Working into ring, ch 1 (counts as first sc), 7 sc. Join with a ss into top of beginning ch-1.
ROUND 2: Make a puff st in first st (do not ch 1 to secure), make another puff st into same st, ch 1 to secure, ch 2, *make 2 puff sts into next st (do not secure with ch 1 in between the two), ch 1 to secure, ch 2. Repeat from * to end. Join with a ss to top of first st. Fasten off. (8 double puff sts)
ROUND 3: Join Light Green into first ch-2 sp, * (1 puff st, ch 1, 1 puff st) into same sp, ch 2. Repeat from * into each ch-2 sp to end. Join with a ss into top of first puff st. Fasten off.

ROUND 4: Join Ivory into first ch-2 sp, [ch 6 (counts as first dc and ch 3), 2 dc, 1 hdc] into same sp, ch 1, 3 hdc into next ch-2 sp, ch 1, * (1 hdc, 2 dc, ch 3, 2 dc, 1 hdc) into next ch-2 sp, ch 1, 3 hdc into next ch-2 sp, ch 1. Repeat from * twice more, (1 hdc, 1 dc) into beginning corner sp. Join with a ss into top of beginning ch-3. Fasten off.

Back
Make 49 squares in total: 24 with Rose Soraya in the center and 25 with Aguarmarina
Base Round: Using Rose Soraya or Aguamarina, ch 4, join with a ss into first ch to make a ring.
ROUND 1: Working into ring, ch 5 (counts as first dc and ch 2), *3 dc, ch 2. Repeat from * twice more, ch 2, 2 dc. Join with a ss into top of beginning ch-3. Fasten off.
ROUND 2: Join Ivory into first ch-2 sp, ch 5 (counts as first dc and ch 2), 3 dc into same sp, ch 1, *(3 dc, ch 2, 3 dc) into next sp, ch 1. Repeat from * twice more, 2 dc into beginning corner sp. Join with a ss into top of beginning ch-3. Fasten off.

Joining Motifs
Front: 5 squares across and 5 squares down.
Use Aguamarina to join. Lay motifs out side by side and right sides up. Beginning with the first 2 squares and starting with the square to your left, insert your hook through the

Key

- Puff Stitch
- **dc** - double crochet
- **ch** - chain
- **hdc** - half double crochet
- **ss** - slip stitch
- **sc** - single crochet

back loop only of the first st, then insert hook into back loop of the first st in the next square, make a sc. Repeat to end. Continue joining the remaining squares this way. When all your squares have been joined across, join each strip of squares together in the same way. Fasten off.

Back: 7 squares across and 7 squares down.
Use Light Green to join. Use the same method as for the front to join.

Join Front and Back Pieces
Using Aguamarina, sc front and back pieces together. Fasten off.

Shell Edging
Join Glicine, ch 1 (counts as first sc), skip next 2 sts, 7 dc into next st, skip next 2 sts, * sc into next st, skip next 2 sts, 7 dc into next st, skip next 2 sts. Repeat from * to end. Join with a ss into top of first ch-1. Fasten off.

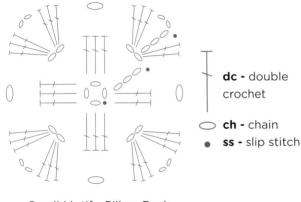

dc - double crochet

ch - chain

ss - slip stitch

Small Motif - Pillow Back

Pillow Front

Finished Size
42 x 42 cm

Pillow Back

Red & White Pillow

Materials

40 x 40 cm fabric for pillow back

Hook: 3.5 mm

DMC Natura Just Cotton: 50g-115m

Colors:

- ○ N 01 Ibiza
- ○ N 03 Sable
- ● N 23 Passion
- ○ N 06 Rose Layette
- ○ N 07 Spring Rose

Puff st: yo, insert hook into st, yo, draw loop up to desired stitch height (3 loops) on hook. Repeat 3 more times into same st, yo, draw through all 9 loops on hook. Ch 1 to secure.

3-Bobble st: yo and insert hook into st, yo, draw loop through, yo, draw through first 2 loops on hook. Repeat 2 more times into same st (4 loops on hook), yo and draw through all loops on hook

Note: The first bobble st in a round is started differently to subsequent bobbles in round. Instructions for the first bobble are included within the pattern. For subsequent bobbles follow the instructions above.

Finished size: 42 x 42 cm

Make 25 squares in total

Base Round: Using Passion ch 4, join with a ss into first ch to make a ring.

ROUND 1: Working into ring, make puff st, ch 2, * make puff st, ch 2. Repeat from * 6 more times. Join with a ss into top of first puff st. Fasten off. (8 puff sts and 8 x ch-2 sps). Make 25.

ROUND 2: Make 13 with Sable and 12 with Rose Layette

Join Rose Layette or Sable into first ch-2 sp, ch 3 (counts as first dc), yo and insert hook into same sp, yo, draw loop through, yo, draw through first 2 loops on hook. Repeat once more into same sp (3 loops on hook), yo and draw through all loops on hook (first 3-bobble st made), ch 3, 3-bobble st) into same sp, ch 1, 3 dc into next sp, ch 1, * (1 x 3-bobble, ch 3, 1 x 3-bobble) in next sp, ch 1, 3 dc in next sp, ch 1. Repeat from * to end. Join with a ss into top of first bobble. Fasten off.

ROUND 3: Join Ibiza into first ch-3 sp, ch 3 (counts as first dc), yo and insert hook into sp, yo, draw loop through, yo, draw through first 2 loops on hook. Repeat once more into same sp (3 loops on hook), yo and draw through all loops on

- ⬭ **3 - Bobble stitch**
- ⬭ **ch -** chain
- ⬭ **Puff Stitch**
- | **dc -** double crochet
- • **ss -** slip stitch

hook (first 3-bobble st made), ch 3, 3-bobble st) into same sp, ch 1, * 2 dc into next ch sp, 2 dc into top of dc sts in previous round, 2 dc into next ch sp, ch 1, (1 x 3-bobble, ch 3, 1 x 3-bobble), ch 1. Repeat from * twice more, 2 dc into next ch sp, 2 dc into top of dc sts in previous round, 2 dc into next ch sp, ch 1. Join with a ss into top of first bobble. Fasten off.

Joining Motifs

Front: 5 squares across and 5 squares down.

Use Spring Rose to join. Lay motifs out side by side and right sides up. Beginning with the first 2 squares and starting with the square to your left, insert your hook through the back loop only of the first st, then insert hook into back loop of the first st in the next square, make a sc. Repeat to end. Continue joining the remaining squares this way. When all your squares have been joined across, join each strip of squares together in the same way. Fasten off.

Border: Using Rose Layette, ch 1 (counts as first sc), sc through back loop only into each st around joined motifs. Join with a ss into beginning ch-1. Fasten off.

Stitch to fabric back of cushion front.

Shell Edging

Join Sable, ch 1 (counts as first sc), skip next 2 sts, 7 dc into next st, skip next 2 sts, * sc into next st, skip next 2 sts, 7 dc into next st, skip next 2 sts. Repeat from * to end. Join with a ss into top of first ch-1. Fasten off.

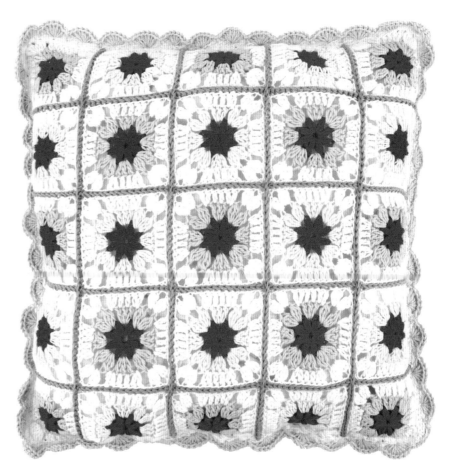

Finished Size
42 x 42 cm

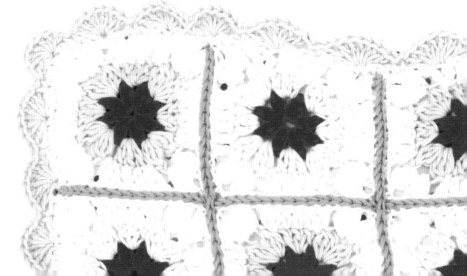

Crochet Trim Pillows

Materials

Fabric for pillow slip
Hook: 3.5 mm
DMC Natura Just Cotton: 50g-115m
Colors:

N 32 Rose Soraya
N 12 Light Green

Crossed double crochet: This stitch is worked over 2 sts. Skip the next st, 1 dc into next st, go back and work 1 dc into skipped st.

5-Bobble st: yo and insert hook into st, yo, draw loop through, yo, draw through first 2 loops on hook. Repeat 4 more times into same st (6 loops on hook), yo and draw through all loops on hook

Note: The first bobble st in a round is started differently to subsequent bobbles in round. Instructions for the first bobble are included within the pattern. For subsequent bobbles follow the instructions above.

Pillow Slip

•Cut 2 pieces of fabric 43 x 45 cm
•Stitch 2 sides and along bottom using a 1cm seam
•Fold open top edge under 2cm. Stitch down.

Finished size: 40 x 45 cm

Pink Trim

Using Rose Soraya sew evenly spaced blanket stitches around pillow-slip opening. Fasten off.

ROW 1: With right side facing, join yarn into first sp between stitches, ch 1 (not counted as a st), 2 sc into same sp, and then in each sp to end. Join with a ss into top of beginning ch-1. Turn

ROW 2: ch 3 (counts as first dc), yo, insert hook into same st, yo, draw up loop, yo, draw through first 2 loops on hook, repeat 3 more times into same sp (5 loops on hook), yo, draw through all 5 loops on hook (first 5-bobble stitch made), * ch 2, skip next 4 sts, make crossed dc, ch 2, skip next 3 sts, make 5-bobble st. Repeat from * to end. Turn.

ROW 3: ch 3, 2 sc in next ch-2 sp, (1 sc, ch 1, 1 sc) into top of crossed dc st in previous row, * 2 sc into next ch-2 sp, ch 2, 2 sc into next ch-2 sp, (1 sc, ch 1, 1 sc) into top of crossed dc st in previous row. Repeat from * to end. Join with a ss into top of beginning ch of previous row.

Green Trim

Using Light Green sew evenly spaced blanket stitches around pillow-slip opening. Fasten off.

ROW 1: With right side facing, join yarn into first sp between stitches, ch 1 (not counted as a st), 2 sc into same sp, and then in each sp to end. Join with a ss into top of beginning ch-1. Turn.

ROW 2: ch 1 (not counted as a stitch), * 1 hdc, ch 1, 1 hdc, ch 1, 1 hdc, ch 1, 1 hdc, ch 1, 1 dc, ch 1, 1 tr, ch 1, 1 tr, ch 1, 1 dc, ch 1. Repeat from * to end. Join with a ss into top of beginning ch-1. Fasten off.

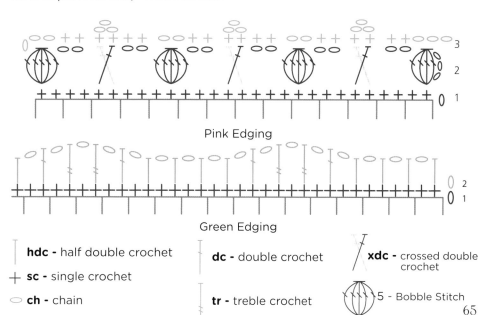

Pink Edging

Green Edging

hdc - half double crochet

sc - single crochet

ch - chain

dc - double crochet

tr - treble crochet

xdc - crossed double crochet

5 - Bobble Stitch

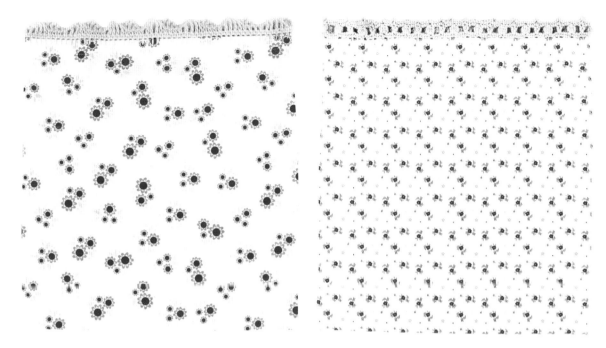

Finished Size

40 x 45 cm

Flower Cushion

Materials

Hook: 3.5 mm
DMC Natura Just Cotton: 50g-115m
Colors:

- N 83 Blé
- N 12 Light Green
- N 76 Bamboo
- N 05 Bleu Layette
- N 06 Rose Layette
- N 32 Rose Soraya
- N 81 Acanthe
- N 47 Safran
- N 25 Aguamarina
- N 30 Glicine
- N 31 Malva
- N 18 Coral
- N 64 Prussian

40 x 40 cm fabric for pillow back

Finished size: 42 x 42 cm

- $+$ **sc -** single crochet
- $\bigcirc$ **ch -** chain
- $\bullet$ **ss -** slip stitch
- **tr -** treble crochet
- **dc -** double crochet

Make 16 squares in total

Base round: ch 4, join with a ss into first ch to make a ring.

ROUND 1: ch 4 (counts as first dc and ch 1), *1 dc, ch 1. Repeat from * 6 more times. Join with a ss into top of beginning ch-3. Fasten off. (8 dc and 8 ch-1 sps)

ROUND 2: Join new color into first ch-1 sp, (ch 3, 2 tr, ch 3, ss) into same ch sp, * (ss, ch 3, 2 tr, ch 3, ss) into next ch-1 sp. Repeat from * into each ch-1 sp to end. Join with a ss into base of beginning ch-3. Fasten off. (8 petals)

ROUND 3: Note: This round will be worked behind the flower petals. Push petals forward to keep them out of the way.
Join new color into top of first dc of Round 1, ch 5 (counts as first sc and ch 4), * sc into top of next dc of Round 1, ch 4. Repeat from * to end. Join with a ss into top of beginning ch-1. (8 ch-4 sps)

ROUND 4: ss into ch sp, [ch 3 (counts as first dc), 2 dc, ch 3, 3 dc] into same sp, ch 1, 3 dc into next sp, ch 1, *(3 dc, ch 3, 3 dc) into next sp, ch 1, 3 dc into next sp, ch 1. Repeat from * to end. Join with a ss into top of beginning ch-3. Fasten off.

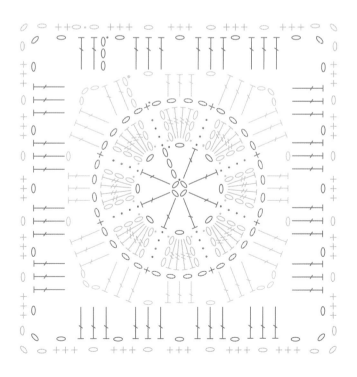

ROUND 5: Join new color into first corner ch-3 sp, [ch 3 (counts as first dc), 2 dc, ch 3, 3 dc] into same sp, ch 1, 3 dc into next sp, ch 1, 3 dc into next sp, ch 1, * (3 dc, ch 3, 3 dc) into next sp, ch 1, 3 dc into next sp, ch 1, 3 dc into next sp, ch 1*. Repeat from * to end. Join with a ss into top of beginning ch-3. Fasten off.

ROUND 6: Join new color first corner ch-3 sp, [ch 1 (counts as first sc), 2 sc, ch 3, 3 sc] into same sp, ch 1, 3 sc, ch 1 into next 3 ch-1 sps, * (3 sc, ch 3, 3 sc) into next corner sp, ch 1, 3 sc, ch 1 into next 3 ch-1 sps. Repeat from * to end. Join with a ss into top of beginning ch-1. Fasten off.

Joining Motifs

4 squares across and 4 squares down.

Use Prussian to join. Lay motifs out side by side and right sides up. Beginning with the first 2 squares and starting with the square to your left, insert your hook through the back loop only of the first st, then insert hook into back loop of the first st in the next square, make a sc. Repeat to end. Continue joining the remaining squares this way. When all your squares have been joined across, join each strip of squares together in the same way.

When all squares have been joined together, sc through the back loop only around the entire piece. Fasten off.

Shell Edging

Join Ble N 83, ch 1 (counts as first sc), skip next 2 sts, 7 dc into next st, skip next 2 sts, * sc into next st, skip next 2 sts, 7 dc into next st, skip next 2 sts. Repeat from * to end. Join with a ss into top of first ch-1. Fasten off.

Finished Size
42 x 42 cm

Dish Cloths

Violet ❀ Green ❀ Turquoise

Violet Dish Cloth

Materials

Hook: 3.5 mm
DMC Natura Just Cotton: 50g-115m
Colors:

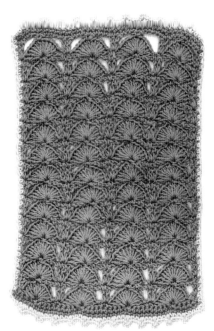

N 33   Amaranto
N 05   Bleu Layette

Finished size: 20 x 30 cm

Foundation Row: Using Amaranto, ch 42
ROW 1: sc into 2nd ch from hook, sc into each ch to end. Ch 1, turn. (41 sc)
ROW 2: sc into each st to end, ch 1, turn
ROW 3: 1 sc into first st, skip next 4 sts, * 12 dc into next st, skip next 4 sts, 1 sc into next st, skip next 4 sts. Repeat from * to last st, 1 sc. Turn.
ROW 4: ch 3 (counts as first dc), 1 dc into same st, * ch 4, sc into center st of shell, ch 4, 2 dc into sc in previous row. Repeat from * to end. Turn.
ROW 5: ch 1 (not counted as a st), * sc into sp between dc-2 in previous row, skip ch-4 of previous row, 12 dc into next st, skip next ch-4. Repeat from * to last st, 1 sc into top of beginning ch of previous row. Turn.

Repeat Rows 4 and 5 to form pattern.

ROW 29: Ch 1 (not counted as a st), * sc between dc-2 of previous round, 4 sc into ch-4 sp, sc into next st, 4 sc into next ch-4 sp. Repeat from * to last st, 1 sc. Turn. (41 sc)
ROW 30: Ch 1 (not counted as a st), sc into each st to end. Fasten off.

Border

Join Bleu Layette into first sc, ch 1 (not counted as a st), * sc into next 2 sts, (1 sc, ch 3, 1 sc) into next st. Repeat from * until end of row. Work 2 sc into corner, sc into each st along the side, 2 sc into corner st. Along bottom row, * sc into next 2 sts, (1 sc, ch 3, 1 sc) into next st. Repeat from * until end of row. Work 2 sc into corner, sc into each st along the side, 2 sc into corner st. Join with a ss into top of beginning ch-1. Fasten off.

Finished Size
20 x 30 cm

⬭ **ch -** chain

✛ **sc -** single crochet

┃ **dc -** double crochet

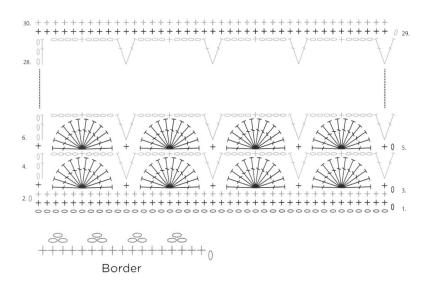

Border

Green Dish Cloth

Materials

Hook: 3.5 mm
DMC Natura Just Cotton: 50g-115m
Colors:

N 76 Bamboo
N 32 Rose Soraya

Finished size: 20 x 33 cm

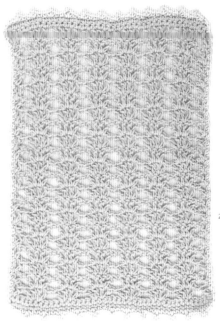

Finished Size
20 x 33 cm

Foundation Row: Using Bamboo, ch 43.

ROW 1: sc into second ch from hook, sc to end. ch 1, turn. (42 sc)
ROW 2: ch 1 (not counted as a st) sc to end. Turn.
ROW 3: ch 4 (counts as first dc and ch 1), dc into same st, skip 4 sts, *(1 dc, ch 1, 1 dc) into next st twice, skip 4 sts. Repeat from * to last st, (1 dc, ch 1, 1 dc) into last st. Turn.
ROW 4: ch 4 (counts as first dc and ch 1), dc into same st, * skip next [ch 1, 2 dc, ch 1] of previous row, (1 dc, ch 1, 1 dc) into next st 2 dc [last and first dcs of clusters in previous row]. Repeat from * to end. Turn

ROWS 5 – 23: Work as for Row 4
ROW 24: ch 1 (not counted as a st), sc into each st to end. Turn.
ROW 25: ch 1 (not counted as a st), sc into each st to end. Fasten off.

Border

Join Rose Soraya into first sc, ch 1 (not counted as a st), * sc into next 2 sts, (1 sc, ch 3, 1 sc) into next st. Repeat from * until end of row. Work 2 sc into corner, sc into each st along the side, 2 sc into corner st. Along bottom row, * sc into next 2 sts, (1 sc, ch 3, 1 sc) into next st. Repeat from * until end of row. Work 2 sc into corner, sc into each st along the side, 2 sc into corner st. Join with a ss into top of beginning ch-1. Fasten off.

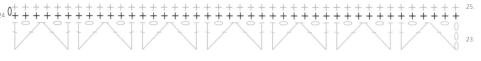

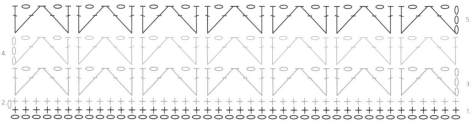

dc - double crochet

ch - chain

sc - single crochet

Border

Turquoise Dish Cloth

Materials

Hook: 3.5 mm
DMC Natura Just Cotton: 50g-115m
Colors:

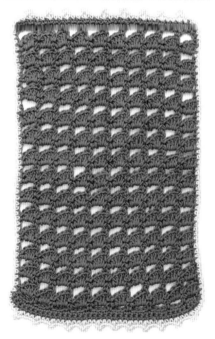

N 64   Prussian
N 81   Acanthe

Finished size: 20 x 33 cm

Foundation Row: Using Prussian, ch 42

ROW 1: sc into second ch from hook, sc into each ch to end. Ch 1, turn. (41 sc)

ROW 2: sc into each st to end. Ch 1, turn.

ROW 3: sc into first st, * ch 3, skip next 3 sts, sc into next st. Repeat from * to end. Turn

ROW 4: Ch 3 (counts as first dc) , (2 dc, 1 hdc, 1 sc) into next ch-3 sp, * 1 sc into next st, ch 3, (2 dc, 1 hdc, 1 sc) into ch sp. Repeat from * to last st, 1 sc. Turn

ROW 5: Ch 6, sc into top of 3rd ch of ch-3 in previous row, * ch 3, sc into top of 3rd ch of ch-3 in previous row. Repeat from * to end. Turn.

ROWS 6 – 31: Repeat Rows 4 and 5 to form pattern.

ROW 32: ch 1 (not counted as a st), * 3 sc into each ch sp, 1 sc into each sc of previous row. Repeat from * to end. ch 1, turn.

ROW 33: sc to end. (41 sc)

Border

Join Acanthe into first sc, ch 1 (not counted as a st), * sc into next 2 sts, (1 sc, ch 3, 1 sc) into next st. Repeat from * until end of row. Work 2 sc into corner, sc into each st along the side, 2 sc into corner st. Along bottom row, * sc into next 2 sts, (1 sc, ch 3, 1 sc) into next st. Repeat from * until end of row. Work 2 sc into corner, sc into each st along the side, 2 sc into corner st. Join with a ss into top of beginning ch-1. Fasten off.

Finished Size
20 x 33 cm

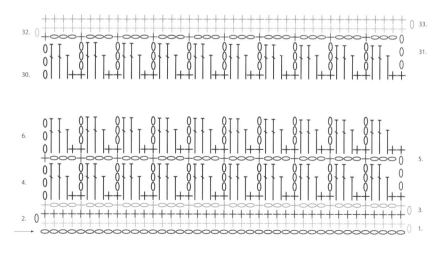

$+$ **sc -** single crochet

dc - double crochet

hdc - half double crochet

⬭ **ch -** chain

Border

Kitchen Towel Edgings

Materials

Fabric

Hook: 3.5 mm
DMC Natura Just Cotton: 50g-115m
Colors:

    N 06   Rose Layette
    N 81   Acanthe
    N 12   Light Green

Finished size: 38 x 50 cm

dc - double crochet

ch - chain

sc - single crochet

Sew fabric rectangle – 36 cm wide x 46 cm long

Pink Edging

Start: Using Rose Layette, sew evenly spaced blanket stitches along top and/or bottom edge/s. Fasten off.
ROW 1: With right side facing, join yarn into first sp between stitches, sc 2 into each sp to end. Make sure your stitch count is a multiple of 4. Fasten off.
ROW 2: Rejoin yarn into first st of Row 1, ch 4 (counts as first dc and ch 1, 1 dc) into same st, ch 1, skip next 4 sts, * sc into next st, ch 1, skip next 4 sts, (1 dc, ch 1, 1 dc, ch 1, 1 dc) into next st, ch 1, skip next 4 sts. Repeat from * to end. Fasten off.

Green Edging

Start: Using Light Green, sew evenly spaced blanket stitches along top and/or bottom edge/s. Fasten off.
ROW 1: With right side facing, join yarn into first sp between stitches, sc 2 into each sp to end. Make sure your stitch count is a multiple of 4. Fasten off.
ROW 2: Rejoin yarn into first st of Row 1, ch 1 (not counted as a st), sc into same st, skip 2 sts, * 5 dc into next st, skip 2 sts, sc into next st, skip 2 sts. Repeat from * to end. Fasten off.

Peach Edging

Start: Using Acanthe, sew evenly spaced blanket stitches along top and/or bottom edge/s. Fasten off.
ROW 1: With right side facing, join yarn into first sp between stitches, sc 2 into each sp to end. Make sure your stitch count is a multiple of 4. Fasten off.
ROW 2: Rejoin yarn into first st of Row 1, ch 4 (counts as first dc and ch 1), dc into same st, ch 2, * skip next 4 sts, (1 dc, ch 1, 1 dc) into next st, ch 2. Repeat from * to end. Turn.
ROW 3: (1 sc, 3 ch, 1 sc) into first ch-1 sp, 1 sc in next ch-2 sp, * (1 sc, 3 ch, 1 sc) into next ch-1 sp, 1 sc into next ch-2 sp. Repeat from * to end. Fasten off.

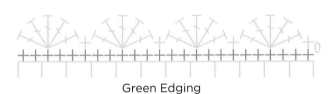

Pink Edging

Green Edging

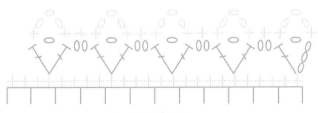

Peach Edging

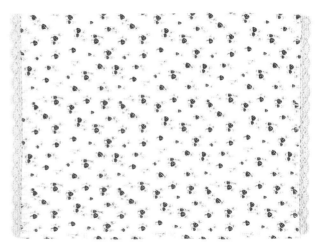

Finished Size
38 x 50 cm

Coasters

Materials

Hook: 3.5 mm
DMC Natura Just Cotton: 50g-115m
Colors:

- N 83 Blé
- N 06 Rose Layette
- N 25 Aguamarina
- N 32 Rose Soraya
- N 31 Malva
- N 47 Safran
- N 81 Acanthe
- N 76 Bamboo
- N 12 Light Green
- N 18 Coral

4-Bobble st: yo and insert hook into st, yo, draw loop through, yo, draw through first 2 loops on hook. Repeat 3 more times into same st (5 loops on hook), yo and draw through all loops on hook.

Note: The first bobble st in a round is started differently to subsequent bobbles in round. Instructions for the first bobble are included within the pattern. For subsequent bobbles follow the instructions above.
Finished size: 12 cm diameter

4 - Bobble Stitch

- **ch -** chain
- **sc -** single crochet
- **ss -** slip stitch

Base Round: Ch 4, join with a ss into first ch to make a ring.
ROUND 1: Working into ring, ch 1 (not counted as a st), 8 sc. Join with a ss into top of beginning ch-1.
ROUND 2: Ch 3 (counts as first dc), yo and insert hook into same st, yo, draw loop through, yo, draw through first 2 loops on hook. Repeat 2 more times into same st (4 loops on hook), yo and draw through all loops on hook (first **4-bobble** made), ch 1, * make 4-bobble in next st, ch 1. Repeat from * to end. Join with a ss into top of beginning ch-3. Fasten off. (8 bobbles).
ROUND 3: Join new color in first ch-1 sp, ch 3 (counts as first dc), yo and insert hook into same st, yo, draw loop through, yo, draw through first 2 loops on hook. Repeat 2 more times into same

st (4 loops on hook), yo and draw through all loops on hook (first **4-bobble** made), ch 1, make another **4-bobble** in same sp), ch 1, *(1 **4-bobble**, ch 1, 1 **4-bobble**) into next sp, ch 1. Repeat from * to end. Join with a ss into top of beginning ch-3. Fasten off.
ROUND 4: Join new color in first ch-1 sp, ch 3 (counts as first dc), yo and insert hook into same st, yo, draw loop through, yo, draw through first 2 loops on hook. Repeat 2 more times into same st (4 loops on hook), yo and draw through all loops on hook (first **4-bobble** made), ch 1, (1 **4-bobble**, ch 1, 1 **4-bobble**) in next sp, ch 1, * 1 **4-bobble** in next sp, ch 1, (1 **4-bobble**, ch 1, 1 **4-bobble**) in next sp, ch 1. Repeat from * to end. Join with a ss into top of beginning ch-3. Fasten off.
ROUND 5: Join new color in first ch-1 sp, ch 1 (counts as first sc), 2 sc into same sp, 3 sc into each sp to end. Join with a ss into top of beginning ch-1. Fasten off.
ROUND 6: Join new color into top of first sc in previous round, ch 1 (counts as first sc), sc into each st to end. Join with a ss into top of beginning ch-1. Fasten off.

Finished Size
12 cm diameter

Ipad Cover

Materials

Hook: 3.5 mm
DMC Natura Just Cotton: 50g-115m
Colors:

- N 12 Light Green
- N 76 Bamboo
- N 32 Rose Soraya
- N 25 Aguamarina
- N 31 Malva

Finished size: 14 x 20 cm

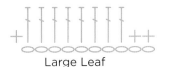
Large Leaf

Small Leaf

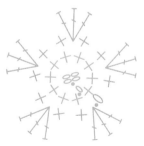
Flower

Foundation Row: Using Light Green, ch 31.
ROW 1: sc into 2nd ch from hook, sc into each ch to end. Turn (30 sc)
ROWS 2 - 92: Ch 1 (not counted as a st), sc into each st to end. Turn. Fasten off after last row.
Finishing: Fold in half and sew sides together.

Shell edging

Join yarn into first st at top with a sc, skip next 2 stitches, 5 dc into next st, skip next 2 sts, * sc into next st, skip next 2 sts, 5 dc into next st, skip next 2 sts. Repeat from * to end. Join with a ss into first sc. Fasten off.

Flowers

Base round: Using Bamboo, ch 4, join with a ss into first ch to make a ring. Make 3.
ROUND 1: Working into ring, ch 1 (not counted as a st), 10 sc. Join with a ss into top of beginning ch-1.
Fasten off.
ROUND 2: Make one each in Aguamarina, Rose Soraya and Malva
Join yarn into first sc of previous round, ch 1 (counts as first sc, 3 dc, 1 sc) into same st, skip next st, * (1 sc, 3 dc, 1 sc) into next st, skip next st. Repeat from * to end. Join with a ss into beginning ch-1. Fasten off. (5 petals)

Small Leaf

Foundation Row: Using Bamboo, ch 8.
ROW 1: Sc into 2nd ch from hook, sc in next ch, dc in next 4 ch, (1 dc, 1 sc) into last ch. Fasten off

Large Leaf

Foundation Row: Using Bamboo, ch 11.
ROW 1: sc into 2nd ch from hook, sc in next ch, dc in next 7 ch, (1 dc, 1 sc) into last ch. Fasten off
Sew the flowers and leaves to the cover.

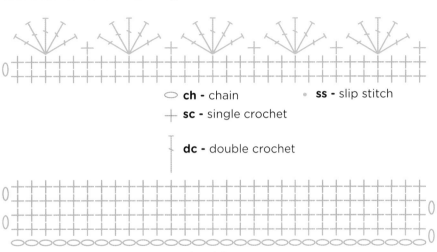

- ⬭ **ch -** chain
- + **sc -** single crochet
- ⊺ **dc -** double crochet
- • **ss -** slip stitch

Ipad Cover

Hangers

Blue Hanger

Materials
Hook: 3.5 mm
DMC Natura Just Cotton: 50g-115m
Colors:

- N 05   Bleu Layette
- N 12   Light Green
- N 32   Rose Soraya
- N 81   Acanthe

Puff st. yo, insert hook into st, yo, draw loop up to desired stitch height (3 loops) on hook. Repeat 3 more times into same st, yo, draw through all 9 loops on hook. Ch 1 to secure.

Finished size:
To fit a 42 cm wooden hanger

Foundation Row: Using Bleu Layette, ch 13.

ROW 1: sc into 2nd ch from hook, sc into each ch to end. Turn. (12 sc)
ROWS 2-9: ch 1 (not counted as a st), sc to end. Turn.
ROW 10: ch 1 (not counted as a st), sc in next 3 sts, change for Rose Soraya, make a puff st, change back to Bleu Layette, sc in next 8 sts. Turn.
ROWS 11-15: ch 1 (not counted as a st), sc to end. Turn.
ROW 16: ch 1 (not counted as a st), sc in next 3 sts, change for Acanthe, make a puff st, change back to Bleu Layette, sc in next 8 sts. Turn.
ROWS 17-21: ch 1 (not counted as a st), sc to end. Turn.
ROW 22: ch 1 (not counted as a st), sc in next 3 sts, change for Light Green, make a puff st, change back to Bleu Layette, sc in next 8 sts. Turn.
ROWS 23 – 76: Repeat this sequence, making a puff st using Rose Soraya in Rows 28, 46 and 64, Acanthe in Rows 34, 52 and 70, Light Green in Rows 40, 58 and 76
ROWS 77 - 86: ch 1 (not counted as a st), sc to end. Turn. Fasten off after last row.
Finishing: Push the hook of the coat hanger through cover between 6th and 7th st in Row 43. Stitch or sc edges together. Fasten off.

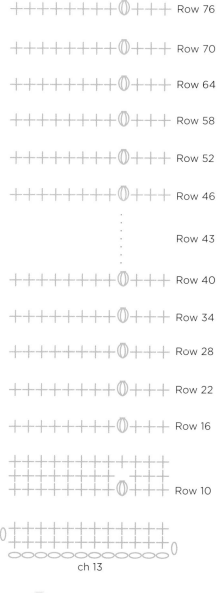

Row 76
Row 70
Row 64
Row 58
Row 52
Row 46
Row 43
Row 40
Row 34
Row 28
Row 22
Row 16
Row 10

ch 13

 Puff Stitch

+ **sc** - single crochet

⬭ **ch** - chain

Yellow Hanger

Materials
Hook: 3.5 mm
DMC Natura Just Cotton: 50g-115m
Colors:

- N 83   Blé
- N 32   Rose Soraya
- N 30   Glicine
- N 01   Ibiza
- N 47   Safran

Popcorn st: 4 dc into same st, remove hook and insert through top of first dc, pull loop through.

Finished size:
To fit a 42 cm wooden hanger

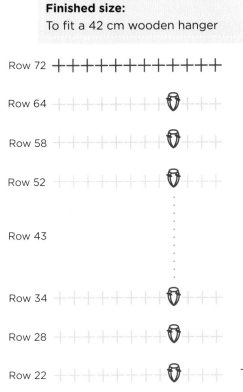

Row 72

Row 64

Row 58

Row 52

Row 43

Row 34

Row 28

Row 22

Row 16

ch 13

+ **sc -** single crochet

pc - popcorn

ch - chain

Foundation Row: Using Blé, ch 13.

ROW 1: sc into 2nd ch from hook, sc into each ch to end. Turn. (12 sc)
ROWS 2-15: ch 1 (not counted as a st), sc to end. Turn.
ROW 16: change color for Safran, ch 1 (not counted as a st), sc to end. Turn.
ROWS 17-21: Change back to Blé, ch 1 (not counted as a st), sc to end. Turn.
ROW 22: ch 1 (not counted as a st), sc in next 3 sts, change for Rose Soraya, make a popcorn st, change back to Blé, sc in next 8 sts. Turn.
ROWS: 23 - 27: ch 1 (not counted as a st), sc to end. Turn.
ROW 28: ch 1 (not counted as a st), sc in next 3 sts, change for Ibiza, make a popcorn st, change back to Blé, sc in next 8 sts. Turn.
ROWS: 29 - 33: ch 1 (not counted as a st), sc to end. Turn.
ROW 34: ch 1 (not counted as a st), sc in next 3 sts, change for Glicine, make a popcorn st, change back to Blé, sc in next 8 sts. Turn.
ROWS: 35 - 51: ch 1 (not counted as a st), sc to end. Turn.

ROW 52: ch 1 (not counted as a st), sc in next 3 sts, change for Glicine, make a popcorn st, change back to Blé, sc in next 8 sts. Turn.
ROWS: 53 - 57: ch 1 (not counted as a st), sc to end. Turn.
ROW 58: ch 1 (not counted as a st), sc in next 3 sts, change for Ibiza, make a popcorn st, change back to Blé, sc in next 8 sts. Turn.
ROWS: 59 - 63: ch 1 (not counted as a st), sc to end. Turn.
ROW 64: ch 1 (not counted as a st), sc in next 3 sts, change for Rose Soraya, make a popcorn st, change back to Blé, sc in next 8 sts. Turn.
ROWS 65- 71: ch 1 (not counted as a st), sc to end. Fasten off. Turn.
ROW 72: Change color for Safran, ch 1 (not counted as a st), sc to end. Turn.
ROWS 73 – 86: Change back to Blé, ch 1 (not counted as a st), sc to end. Turn. Fasten off after last row.
Finishing: Push the hook of the coat hanger through cover between 6th and 7th st in Row 43. Stitch or sc edges together. Fasten off.

90

Ivory Hanger

Materials
Hook: 3.5 mm
DMC Natura Just Cotton: 50g-115m
Colors:

N 02 Ivory
N 32 Rose Soraya
N 12 Light Green
N 23 Passion

Finished size:
To fit a 42 cm wooden hanger

Foundation Row: Using Ivory, ch 13.

ROW 1: sc into 2nd ch from hook, sc into each ch to end. Turn. (12 sc)
ROWS 2-17: ch 1 (not counted as a st), sc to end. Turn.
ROW 18: Change color for Passion, ch 1 (not counted as a st), sc to end. Turn.
ROWS 19-20: change color for Ivory, ch 1 (not counted as a st), sc to end. Turn.
ROW 21: Change color for Passion, ch 1 (not counted as a st), sc to end. Turn.
ROWS 22 - 23: Change color for Ivory, ch 1 (not counted as a st), sc to end. Turn.
ROW 24: Change color for Passion, ch 1 (not counted as a st), sc to end. Turn. Fasten off.
ROWS 25 - 70: Change color for Ivory, ch 1 (not counted as a st), sc to end. Turn. Fasten off after last row.
ROWS 71-80: Change color for Light Green, ch 1 (not counted as a st), sc to end. Turn. Fasten off.
Finishing: Push the hook of the coat hanger through cover between 6th and 7th st in Row 43. Sc edges together using Rose Soraya. Fasten off

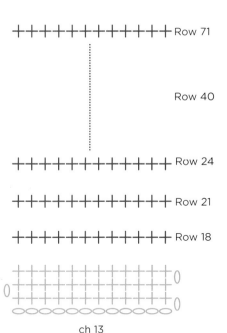

+ **sc -** single crochet

◯ **ch -** chain

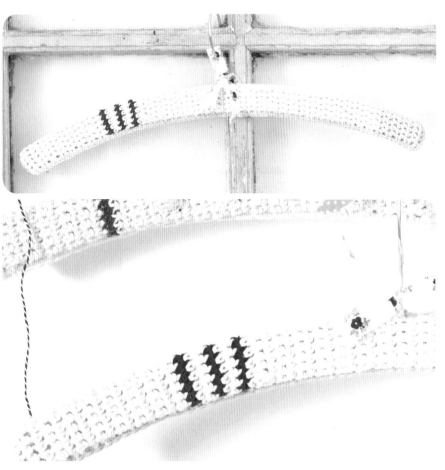

Shawl

Materials

Hook: 4 mm
DMC Natura Just Cotton: 50g-115m
Colors:

N 02	Ivory
N 83	Blé
N 06	Rose Layette
N 03	Sable

Finished size: 150 cm x 118 cm

Base Round: Using Sable, ch 4, join with a ss into first ch to make a ring.
ROW 1: ch 3 (counts as first dc), 3 dc, ch 3, dc 4 into ring. Turn.
ROUND 2: ch 3 (counts as first dc), 3 dc into same st, ch 2, (3 dc, ch 3, 3 dc) into next sp, ch 2, 4 dc into top of beginning ch of previous row. Turn.
ROUND 3: ch 3 (counts as first dc), 3 dc into same st, ch 2, 3 dc into next sp, ch 2, (3 dc, ch 3, 3 dc) into next sp, ch 2, dc 3 into next sp, ch 2, 4 dc into top of beginning ch of previous row. Turn.
ROUND 4: ch 3 (counts as first dc), 3 dc into same st, ch 2, 3 dc, ch 2 into next 2 sps, (3 dc, ch 3, 3 dc) into next sp, ch 2, 3 dc, ch 2 into next 2 sps, 4 dc into top of beginning ch of previous row. Turn.

ROUNDS 5 - 34: Continue working this way, changing color to Rose Layette in Rows 12, 16, 24 and 28, Ivory in Rows 20 and 29 and Blé in Row 33
ROW 35: Using Rose Soraya ch 1 (counts as first sc), 3 sc into same st, * ch 2, 3 sc into next ch-2 sp. Repeat from * into each ch-2 sp along shawl side and (3 sc, ch 3, 3 sc) into centre ch-3 sp, * ch 2, 3 sc into next ch-2 sp. Repeat from * into each ch-2 sp along side, 4 sc into top of beginning ch of previous round.
ROW 36: Using Blé, work the same as Row 35. Fasten off.

Finishing: (optional) attach tassels in each corner.

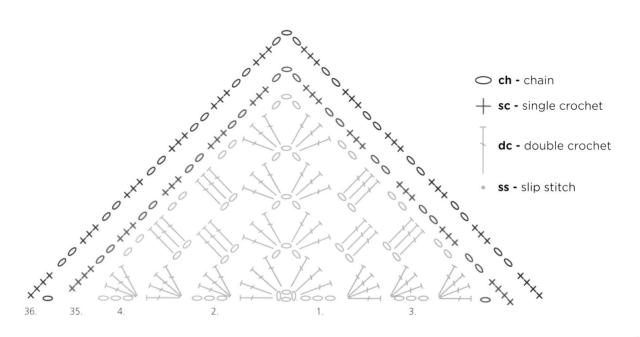

⬭	**ch** - chain
+	**sc** - single crochet
⊤	**dc** - double crochet
•	**ss** - slip stitch

36. 35. 4. 2. 1. 3.

Finished Size
150cm x 118 cm

Colorful Stripe Blanket

Materials

Hook: 4 mm
DMC Natura Just Cotton: 50g-115m
Colors:

N 05 Bleu Layette
N 02 Ivory
N 83 Blé
N 12 Light Green
N 06 Rose Layette
N 32 Rose Soraya
N 81 Acanthe
N 30 Glicine

Borders colors:

N 47 Safran
N 23 Passion

3-Bobble st: yo and insert hook into st, yo, draw loop through, yo, draw through first 2 loops on hook. Repeat 2 more times into same st (4 loops on hook), yo and draw through all loops on hook.

Finished size: 85 x 95 cm

Foundation Row: Using Acanthe, ch 130.

ROW 1: sc into 2nd ch from hook, sc into each ch. Turn. (129 sc)

ROW 2: ch 3 (counts as first dc), dc into each st to end. Fasten off.

ROW 3: Join Rose Layette, ch 1 (not counted as a st), sc into same st, * ch 3, skip 2 sts, make a 3-bobble st, ch 3, skip 2 sts, sc into next st. Repeat from * to end. Fasten off. Turn.

ROW 4: Join Ivory, ch 5 (counts as first dc and ch 2), sc into top of bobble in previous row, ch 2, dc into top of sc in previous row, * ch 2, sc into top of bobble in previous row, ch 2, dc into top of sc in previous row. Repeat from * to end. Turn.

ROW 5: ch 3 (counts as first dc), * 2 dc into next ch sp, dc into top of sc in previous row, 2 dc into next ch sp, dc into top of dc in previous row. Repeat from * to end. Fasten off. Turn.

ROW 6: Join Glicine, ch 1 (not counted as a st), sc into same st, * ch 3, skip 2 sts, make a 3-bobble st, ch 3, skip 2 sts, sc into next st. Repeat from * to end. Fasten off. Turn

ROW 7: Join Acanthe, ch 5 (counts as first dc and ch 2), sc into top of bobble in previous row, ch 2, dc into top of sc in previous row, * ch 2, sc into top of bobble in previous row, ch 2, dc into top of sc in previous row. Repeat from * to end. Turn.

ROW 8: ch 3 (counts as first dc), * 2 dc into next ch sp, dc into top of sc in previous row, 2 dc into next ch sp, dc into top of dc in previous row. Repeat from * to end. Fasten off. Turn.

ROW 9: Join Light Green, ch 1 (not counted as a st), sc into same st, * ch 3, skip 2 sts, make a 3-bobble st, ch 3, skip 2 sts, sc into next st. Repeat from * to end. Fasten off. Turn.

ROW 10: Join Ivory ch 5 (counts as first dc and ch 2), sc into top of bobble in previous row, ch 2, dc into top of sc in previous row, * ch 2, sc into top of bobble in previous row, ch 2, dc into top of sc in previous row. Repeat from * to end. Turn.

3 - Bobble stitch

dc - double crochet

ch - chain

sc - single crochet

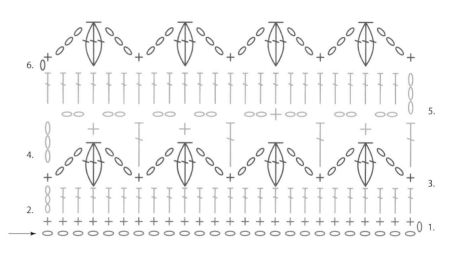

ROW 11: ch 3 (counts as first dc), * 2 dc into next ch sp, dc into top of sc in previous row, 2 dc into next ch sp, dc into top of dc in previous row. Repeat from * to end. Fasten off. Turn.

ROW 12: Join Bleu Layette, ch 1 (not counted as a st), sc into same st, * ch 3, skip 2 sts, make a 3-bobble st, ch 3, skip 2 sts, sc into next st. Repeat from * to end. Fasten off. Turn.

ROW 13: Join Acanthe, ch 5 (counts as first dc and ch 2), sc into top of bobble in previous row, ch 2, dc into top of sc in previous row, * ch 2, sc into top of bobble in previous row, ch 2, dc into top of sc in previous row. Repeat from * to end. Turn.

ROW 14: ch 3 (counts as first dc), * 2 dc into next ch sp, dc into top of sc in previous row, 2 dc into next ch sp, dc into top of dc in previous row. Repeat from * to end. Fasten off. Turn.

ROW 15: Join Glicine, ch 1 (not counted as a st), sc into same st, * ch 3, skip 2 sts, make a 3-bobble st, ch 3, skip 2 sts, sc into next st. Repeat from * to end. Fasten off. Turn.

ROW 16: Join Ivory, ch 5 (counts as first dc and ch 2), sc into top of bobble in previous row, ch 2, dc into top of sc in previous row, * ch 2, sc into top of bobble in previous row, ch 2, dc into top of sc in previous row. Repeat from * to end. Turn.

ROW 17: ch 3 (counts as first dc), * 2 dc into next ch sp, dc into top of sc in previous row, 2 dc into next ch sp, dc into top of dc in previous row. Repeat from * to end. Fasten

off. Turn.

ROW 18: Join Blé, ch 1 (not counted as a st), sc into same st, * ch 3, skip 2 sts, make a 3-bobble st, ch 3, skip 2 sts, sc into next st. Repeat from * to end. Fasten off. Turn.

ROW 19: Join Ivory ch 5 (counts as first dc and ch 2), sc into top of bobble in previous row, ch 2, dc into top of sc in previous row, * ch 2, sc into top of bobble in previous row, ch 2, dc into top of sc in previous row. Repeat from * to end. Turn.

ROW 20: ch 3 (counts as first dc), * 2 dc into next ch sp, dc into top of sc in previous row, 2 dc into next ch sp, dc into top of dc in previous row. Repeat from * to end. Fasten off. Turn.

ROW 21: Join Rose Soraya, ch 1 (not counted as a st), sc into same st, * ch 3, skip 2 sts, make a 3-bobble st, ch 3, skip 2 sts, sc into next st. Repeat from * to end. Fasten off. Turn.

ROW 22: Join Acanthe, ch 5 (counts as first dc and ch 2), sc into top of bobble in previous row, ch 2, dc into top of sc in previous row, * ch 2, sc into top of bobble in previous row, ch 2, dc into top of sc in previous row. Repeat from * to end. Turn.

ROW 23: ch 3 (counts as first dc), * 2 dc into next ch sp, dc into top of sc in previous row, 2 dc into next ch sp, dc into top of dc in previous row. Repeat from * to end. Fasten off. Turn.

ROW 24: Join Light Green, ch 1 (not counted as a st), sc into same st, * ch 3, skip 2 sts, make a 3-bobble st, ch 3, skip 2 sts, sc into next st. Re-

peat from * to end. Fasten off. Turn

ROW 25: Join Ivory, ch 5 (counts as first dc and ch 2), sc into top of bobble in previous row, ch 2, dc into top of sc in previous row, * ch 2, sc into top of bobble in previous row, ch 2, dc into top of sc in previous row. Repeat from * to end. Turn.

ROW 26: ch 3 (counts as first dc), * 2 dc into next ch sp, dc into top of sc in previous row, 2 dc into next ch sp, dc into top of dc in previous row. Repeat from * to end. Fasten off. Turn.

ROW 27: Join Glicine, ch 1 (not counted as a st), sc into same st. * ch 3, skip 2 sts, make a 3-bobble st, ch 3, skip 2 sts, sc into next st. Repeat from * to end. Fasten off. Turn.

ROW 28: Join Acanthe, ch 5 (counts as first dc and ch 2), sc into top of bobble in previous row, ch 2, dc into top of sc in previous row, * ch 2, sc into top of bobble in previous row, ch 2, dc into top of sc in previous row. Repeat from * to end. Turn.

ROW 29: Ch 3 (counts as first dc), * 2 dc into next ch sp, dc into top of sc in previous row, 2 dc into next ch sp, dc into top of dc in previous row. Repeat from * to end. Fasten off. Turn.

ROW 30: Join Bleu Layette, ch 1 (not counted as a st), sc into same st, * ch 3, skip 2 sts, make a 3-bobble st, ch 3, skip 2 sts, sc into next st. Repeat from * to end. Fasten off. Turn.

ROW 31: Join Acanthe, ch 5 (counts as first dc and ch 2), sc into top of bobble in previous row, ch 2, dc into top of sc in previous row, * ch 2, sc

into top of bobble in previous row, ch 2, dc into top of sc in previous row. Repeat from * to end. Turn.

ROW 32: ch 3 (counts as first dc), * 2 dc into next ch sp, dc into top of sc in previous row, 2 dc into next ch sp, dc into top of dc in previous row. Repeat from * to end. Fasten off. Turn.

ROW 33: Join Rose Layette, ch 1 (not counted as a st), sc into same st, * ch 3, skip 2 sts, make a 3-bobble st, ch 3, skip 2 sts, sc into next st. Repeat from * to end. Fasten off. Turn.

ROW 34: Join Ivory, ch 5 (counts as first dc and ch 2), sc into top of bobble in previous row, ch 2, dc into top of sc in previous row, * ch 2, sc into top of bobble in previous row, ch 2, dc into top of sc in previous row. Repeat from * to end. Turn.

ROW 35: ch 3 (counts as first dc), * 2 dc into next ch sp, dc into top of sc in previous row, 2 dc into next ch sp, dc into top of dc in previous row. Repeat from * to end. Fasten off. Turn.

ROW 36: Join Glicine, ch 1 (not counted as a st), sc into same st, * ch 3, skip 2 sts, make a 3-bobble st, ch 3, skip 2 sts, sc into next st. Repeat from * to end. Fasten off. Turn.

ROW 37: Join Acanthe ch 5 (counts as first dc and ch 2), sc into top of bobble in previous row, ch 2, dc into top of sc in previous row, * ch 2, sc into top of bobble in previous row, ch 2, dc into top of sc in previous row. Repeat from * to end. Turn.

ROW 38: ch 3 (counts as first dc), * 2 dc into next ch sp, dc into top

of sc in previous row, 2 dc into next ch sp, dc into top of dc in previous row. Repeat from * to end. Fasten off. Turn.

ROW 39: Join Light Green, ch 1 (not counted as a st), sc into same st, * ch 3, skip 2 sts, make a 3-bobble st, ch 3, skip 2 sts, sc into next st. Repeat from * to end. Fasten off. Turn.

ROW 40: Join Ivory ch 5 (counts as first dc and ch 2), sc into top of bobble in previous row, ch 2, dc into top of sc in previous row, * ch 2, sc into top of bobble in previous row, ch 2, dc into top of sc in previous row. Repeat from * to end. Turn.

ROW 41: ch 3 (counts as first dc), * 2 dc into next ch sp, dc into top of sc in previous row, 2 dc into next ch sp, dc into top of dc in previous row. Repeat from * to end. Fasten off. Turn.

ROW 42: Join Blé, ch 1 (does not count as a st), sc into same st, * ch 3, skip 2 sts, make a 3-bobble st, ch 3, skip 2 sts, sc into next st. Repeat from * to end. Fasten off. Turn.

ROW 43: Join Ivory, ch 5 (counts as first dc and ch 2), sc into top of bobble in previous row, ch 2, dc into top of sc in previous row, * ch 2, sc into top of bobble in previous row, ch 2, dc into top of sc in previous row. Repeat from * to end. Turn.

ROW 44: Ch 3 (counts as first dc), * 2 dc into next ch sp, dc into top of sc in previous row, 2 dc into next ch sp, dc into top of dc in previous row. Repeat from * to end. Fasten off. Turn.

ROW 45: Join Rose Soraya, ch 1 (does not count as a st), sc into

same st, * ch 3, skip 2 sts, make a 3-bobble st, ch 3, skip 2 sts, sc into next st. Repeat from * to end. Fasten off. Turn.

ROW 46: Join Acanthe, ch 5 (counts as first dc and ch 2), sc into top of bobble in previous row, ch 2, dc into top of sc in previous row, * ch 2, sc into top of bobble in previous row, ch 2, dc into top of sc in previous row. Repeat from * to end. Turn.

ROW 47: Ch 3 (counts as first dc), * 2 dc into next ch sp, dc into top of sc in previous row, 2 dc into next ch sp, dc into top of dc in previous row. Repeat from * to end. Fasten off. Turn.

ROW 48: Join Glicine, ch 1 (not counted as a st), sc into same st, * ch 3, skip 2 sts, make a 3-bobble st, ch 3, skip 2 sts, sc into next st. Repeat from * to end. Fasten off. Turn.

ROW 49: Join Ivory, ch 5 (counts as first dc and ch 2), sc into top of bobble in previous row, ch 2, dc into top of sc in previous row, * ch 2, sc into top of bobble in previous row, ch 2, dc into top of sc in previous row. Repeat from * to end. Turn.

ROW 50: Ch 3 (counts as first dc), * 2 dc into next ch sp, dc into top of sc in previous row, 2 dc into next ch sp, dc into top of dc in previous row. Repeat from * to end. Fasten off. Turn.

ROW 51: Join Bleu Layette, ch 1 (not counted as a st), sc into same st, * ch 3, skip 2 sts, make a 3-bobble st, ch 3, skip 2 sts, sc into next st. Repeat from * to end. Fasten off. Turn.

ROW 52: Join Acanthe, ch 5 (counts as first dc and ch 2), sc into top of bobble in previous row, ch 2, dc into top of sc in previous row, * ch 2, sc into top of bobble in previous row, ch 2, dc into top of sc in previous row. Repeat from * to end. Turn.

ROW 53: ch 3 (counts as first dc), * 2 dc into next ch sp, dc into top of sc in previous row, 2 dc into next ch sp, dc into top of dc in previous row. Repeat from * to end. Fasten off. Turn.

ROW 54: Join Rose Soraya, ch 1 (not counted as a st), sc into same st, * ch 3, skip 2 sts, make a 3-bobble st, ch 3, skip 2 sts, sc into next st. Repeat from * to end.
Fasten off. Turn.

ROW 55: Join Ivory, ch 5 (counts as first dc and ch 2), sc into top of bobble in previous row, ch 2, dc into top of sc in previous row, * ch 2, sc into top of bobble in previous row, ch 2, dc into top of sc in previous row. Repeat from * to end. Turn.

ROW 56: ch 3 (counts as first dc), * 2 dc into next ch sp, dc into top of sc in previous row, 2 dc into next ch sp, dc into top of dc in previous row. Repeat from * to end. Fasten off. Turn.

ROW 57: Join Blé, ch 1 (not counted as a st), sc into same st, * ch 3, skip 2 sts, make a 3-bobble st, ch 3, skip 2 sts, sc into next st. Repeat from * to end. Fasten off. Turn.

ROW 58: Join Ivory, ch 5 (counts as first dc and ch 2), sc into top of bobble in previous row, ch 2, dc into top of sc in previous row, * ch 2, sc into top of bobble in previous row, ch 2, dc into top of sc in previous

row. Repeat from * to end. Turn.

ROW 59: ch 3 (counts as first dc), * 2 dc into next ch sp, dc into top of sc in previous row, 2 dc into next ch sp, dc into top of dc in previous row. Repeat from * to end. Fasten off. Turn.

ROW 60: Join Glicine, ch 1 (not counted as a st), sc into same st, * ch 3, skip 2 sts, make a 3-bobble st, ch 3, skip 2 sts, sc into next st. Repeat from * to end. Fasten off. Turn.

ROW 61: Join Acanthe, ch 5 (counts as first dc and ch 2), sc into top of bobble in previous row, ch 2, dc into top of sc in previous row, * ch 2, sc into top of bobble in previous row, ch 2, dc into top of sc in previous row. Repeat from * to end. Turn.

ROW 62: ch 3 (counts as first dc), * 2 dc into next ch sp, dc into top of sc in previous row, 2 dc into next ch sp, dc into top of dc in previous row. Repeat from * to end. Fasten off. Turn.

ROW 63: ch 1 (not counted as a stitch), sc into ea st to end. Fasten off.

Border

ROW 1: Starting in a corner st, join Ivory, * (1 sc, ch 1, 1 sc) into same st, sc into each st up to next corner. Repeat from * to end. Fasten off.
ROW 2: Join Passion, work the same as for Row 1.
ROW 3: Join Ivory, work the same as for Row 1.

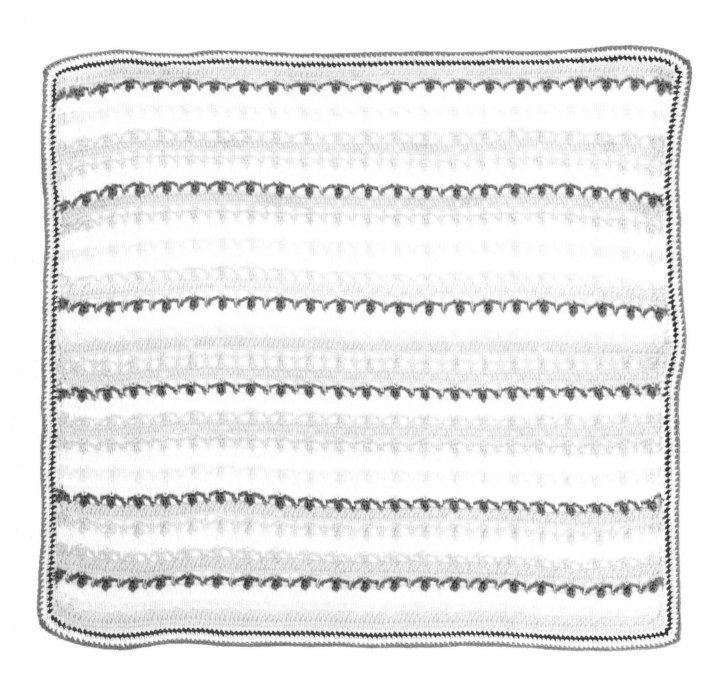

Finished Size
85 x 95 cm

Scarf

Materials

Hook: 3.5 mm

DMC Natura Just Cotton: 50g-115m

Colors:

    N 05 Bleu Layette

    N 02 Ivory

Popcorn st: 4 dc into same st, remove hook and insert through top of first dc, pull loop through.

Finished size: 18 x 150 cm

⬯ **ch -** chain

+ **sc -** single crochet

| **dc -** double crochet

🪶 **pc -** popcorn

Foundation Row: Using Bleu Layette, ch 38.

ROW 1: sc into 2nd ch from hook, sc into each ch to end. Turn. (37 sc)

ROW 2: Ch 1 (not counted as a st), sc into same st, * ch 2, skip 2 sts, sc into next st. Repeat from * to end. Turn.

ROW 3: Ch 3 (counts as first dc), dc into same st, * skip ch-2 sp of previous row, 3 dc into top of sc in previous row. Repeat from * 6 more times. Make a popcorn st into top of next sc in previous row, * skip next ch-2 sp of previous row, 3 dc into top of next sc in previous row. Repeat from * 2 more times, skip next ch-2 sp, 2 dc into top of last st. Turn.

ROW 4: Ch 1 (not counted as a st), sc into same st, * ch 2, sc into centre st of 3-dc in previous row (and into top of popcorn st when you reach it). Repeat from * to end. Turn.

ROW 5: Ch 3 (counts as first dc), dc into same st, * skip ch-2 sp of previous row, 3 dc into top of sc in previous row. Repeat from * 2 more times. Make a popcorn st into top of next sc in previous row, * skip next ch-2 sp of previous row, 3 dc into top of next sc in previous row. Repeat from * 6 more times, skip next ch-2 sp, 2 dc into top of last st. Turn.

ROW 6: Ch 1 (not counted as a st), sc into same st, * ch 2, sc into centre st of 3-dc in previous row (and into top of popcorn st when you reach it). Repeat from * to end. Turn.

ROW 7: Ch 3 (counts as first dc), dc into same st, * skip ch-2 sp of previous row, 3 dc into top of sc in previous row. Repeat from * 8 more times. Make a popcorn st into top of next sc in previous row, skip next ch-2 sp of previous row, 3 dc into top of next sc in previous row, skip next ch-2 sp, 2 dc into top of last st. Turn.

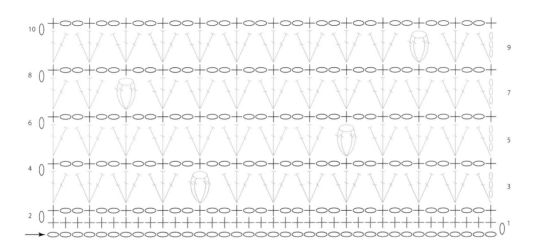

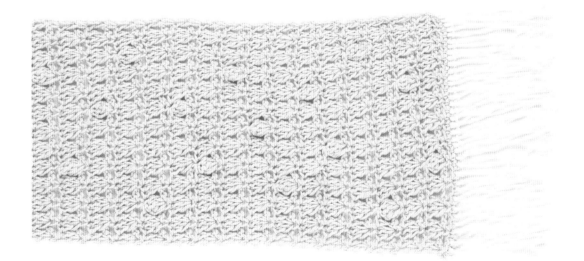

ROW 8: ch 1 (not counted as a st), sc into same st, * ch 2, sc into centre st of 3-dc in previous row (and into top of popcorn st when you reach it). Repeat from * to end. Turn.

ROW 9: ch 3 (counts as first dc), dc into same st, * skip ch-2 sp of previous row, 3 dc into top of sc in previous row. Make a popcorn st into top of next sc in previous row, * skip next ch-2 sp of previous row, 3 dc into top of next sc in previous row. Repeat from * 8 more times, skip next ch-2 sp, 2 dc into top of last st. Turn.

ROWS 10 - 137: Pattern is formed by Rows 2 – 9. Repeat these rows to end. Turn.

ROWS 138 - 139: ch 1 (not counted as a st), sc into each st to end. Fasten off after last row.

Finishing: Add a fringe using Ivory into each st along both ends.

Flower Blanket

Materials

Hook: 3.5 mm

DMC Natura Just Cotton: 50g-115m

Colors:

- ● N 25 Aguamarina- 6 balls

Flowers:

- N 05 Bleu Layette
- ○ N 02 Ivory
- N 83 Blé
- N 12 Light Green
- N 06 Rose Layette
- ● N 32 Rose Soraya
- N 36 Gardenia
- ● N 37 Canelle

Border:

- N 05 Bleu Layette
- ● N 32 Rose Soraya
- N 02 Ivory
- ● N 18 Coral

Joining motifs:

- ○ N 83 Blé
- N 12 Light Green
- N 06 Rose Layette
- ● N 32 Rose Soraya

Popcorn st: 4 dc into same st, remove hook and insert through top of first dc, pull loop through.

Note: The first popcorn st in a round is started differently to subsequent popcorn sts in round. Instructions for the first popcorn are included within the pattern. For subsequent popcorns follow the instructions above.

Finished size: 90 x 110 cm

Square: 10 cm

Base Round: Ch 4, join with a ss into first ch to make a ring.

ROUND 1: Working into ring, ch 1 (not counted as a st), 8 sc. Join with a ss into top of beginning ch-1.

ROUND 2: Ch 3 (counts as first dc), 3 dc into same st, remove hook from loop and insert through top of beginning ch-3, pull loop through (first popcorn st made), ch 2, * make popcorn st in next st, ch 2. Repeat from * to end. Join with a ss into top of first popcorn st. Fasten off. (8 popcorn sts)

Make 80 flowers in total: 10 each in all of the 8 colors.

ROUND 3: Join Aguamarina into first ch-2 sp of previous round, ch 5 (counts as first dc and ch 2), (2 dc, 1 hdc) into same sp, ch 1, 3 dc into next ch-2 sp, ch 1, * (1 hdc, 2 dc, ch 2, 2 dc, 1 hdc) into next ch-2 sp, ch 1, 3 dc into next ch-2 sp, ch 1. Repeat from * twice more, (1 hdc, 1 dc) into beginning corner sp. Join with a ss into top of beginning ch-3.

ROUND 4: ss into corner ch-2 sp, ch 3, (counts as first dc), (2 dc, ch 2, 3 dc) into same sp, ch 1, 3 dc into next sp, ch 1, 3 dc into next sp, ch 1, * (3 dc, ch 2, 3 dc) into next sp, ch 1, 3 dc into next sp, ch 1, 3 dc into next sp, ch 1. Repeat from * to end. Join with a ss into top of beginning ch-3. Fasten off.

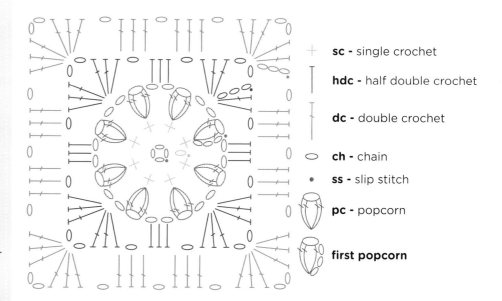

+	**sc -** single crochet
│	**hdc -** half double crochet
†	**dc -** double crochet
⌒	**ch -** chain
•	**ss -** slip stitch
	pc - popcorn
	first popcorn

Joining Motifs

8 squares across and 10 squares down.

Use a different color for each row of joining, choosing from Spring Rose, Blé, Light Green, Rose Layette and Rose Soraya.

Hold 2 square wrong sides facing together (right sides facing out), sc through all sts, continuing joining squares this way until you have reached the end of the strip. Fasten off and join next strip with a different colour. Join all strips together in the same way, using a different color for each row. Fasten off.

Border

ROW 1: Join Bleu Layette into corner sp, * (1 sc, ch 2, 1 sc) into same space, sc into each st up to next corner. Repeat from * to end. Join with a ss into first sc. Fasten off.
ROW 2: Join Rose Soraya. Work as for Row 1.
ROW 3: Join Ivory. Work as for Row 1.
ROW 4: Join Safran. Work as for Row 1.

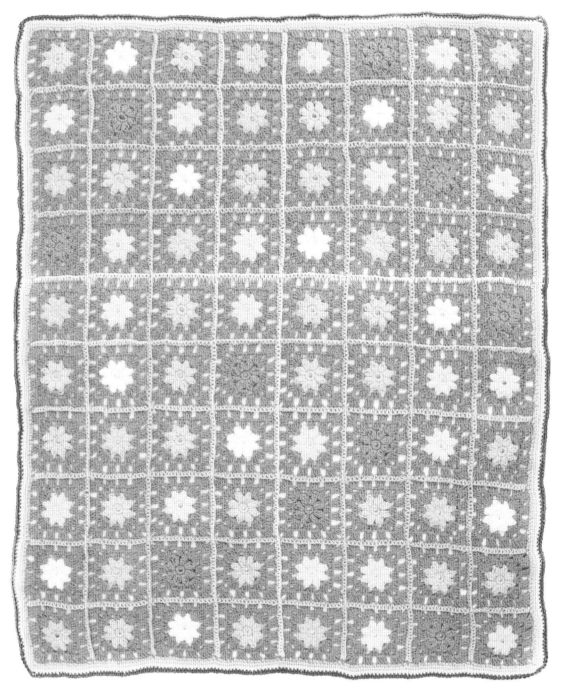

Finished Size
90 x 110 cm

Triangle Garland

Materials

Hook: 3.5 mm
DMC Natura Just Cotton: 50g-115m
Colors:

- N 23 Passion
- N 01 Ibiza
- N 12 Light Green
- N 05 Bleu Layette
- N 32 Rose Soraya
- N 25 Aguamarina
- N 64 Prussian

Finished size:
12 cm triangle
180 cm long

Make 6 triangles in total in the following color sequences:

1. Aguamarina / Passion / Ibiza
2. Aguamarina / Ibiza / Passion
3. Light Green / Passion / Ibiza
4. Light Green / Ibiza / Passion
5. Rose Soraya / Passion / Ibiza
6. Rose Soraya / Ibiza / Passion

Base Round: ch 4, join with a ss into first ch to make a ring. Make 2 each in Aguamarina, Light Green and Rose Soraya

ROUND 1: Working into ring, ch 5 (counts as first dc and ch 2), * 1 dc, ch 2. Repeat from * 4 more times. Join with a ss into top of beginning ch-3. Fasten off.

ROUND 2: Join Passion or Ibiza into first ch-2 sp, (ch 3, 3 tr, ch 3, ss) into same sp. *(ss, ch 3, 3 tr, ch 3, ss) into next sp. Repeat from * into each sp to end. Join with a ss into base of beginning ch-3. Fasten off.

ROUND 3: Join Passion or Ibiza into centre st of first petal, ch 6 (counts as first dc and ch 3), dc into same st, *ch 3, hdc into st between petals, ch 3, sc into centre stitch of next petal, ch 3, hdc into next st between petals, ch 3, (1 dc, ch 3, 1 dc) into centre stitch of next petal. Repeat from * once more, ch 3, hdc into st between next petal, ch 3, sc into centre stitch of next petal, ch 3, hdc into st between next petal, ch 3. Join with a ss into 3rd ch of beginning ch.

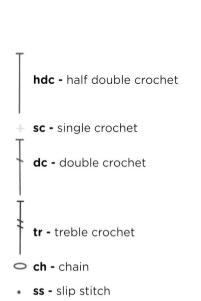

hdc - half double crochet

sc - single crochet

dc - double crochet

tr - treble crochet

ch - chain

ss - slip stitch

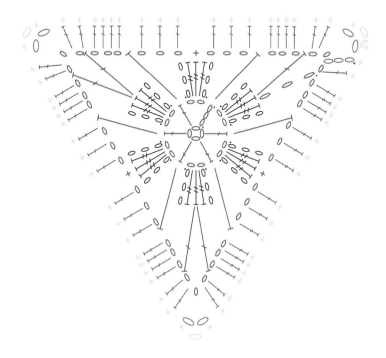

ROUND 4: ss into ch-3 sp, ch 5 (counts as first dc and ch 2,) 2 dc in same sp, * 4 dc in next ch-3 sp, 3 dc in next 2 ch-3 sps, 4 dc in next ch-3 sp, (2 dc, ch 2, 2 dc) in next ch-3 sp (corner). Repeat from * once more, 4 dc in next ch-3 sp, 3 dc in next 2 ch-3 sps, 4 dc in next ch-3 sp, 1 dc in beginning corner sp. Join with a ss into top of beginning ch-3.

ROUND 5: Join (Prussian for white triangle and Bleu Layette for red triangle) into first corner sp, ch 2 (counts as first sc and ch 1), sc into same sp, * sc into each st up to next corner sp, (1 sc, ch 1, 1 sc) into sp. Repeat from * once more, sc into each st to end. Join with a ss into top of beginning ch-1.

Finishing: Using Ibiza, ch 50, join red triangle with sc along the top, ch 10, join white triangle. Continue joining triangle motifs this way to end, ch 50. Fasten off.

Finished Size
12 cm triangle
180 cm long

115

Mittens

Materials

Hook: 3.5 mm
DMC Natura Just Cotton: 50g-115m
Colors:

- N 02 Ivory
- N 83 Blé
- N 06 Rose Layette
- N 81 Acanthe
- N 25 Aguamarina
- N 03 Sable
- N 18 Coral

Finished size: 20 cm diameter /24 cm length

Base Round: Using Safran, ch 31, join with a ss into first ch to make a ring.

ROUND 1: sc into 2nd ch from hook, sc into each ch to end. Join with a ss into top of beginning ch. Fasten off. (30 sc)

ROUND 2: Join Rose Layette, ch 3 (counts as first dc), dc into each st to end. Join with a ss into top of beginning ch-3. Fasten off.

ROUND 3: Join Sable, ch 1 (counts as first sc), sc into each st to end. Join with a ss into top of beginning ch-1.

ROUND 4: Ch 1 (counts as first sc), sc into each st to end. Join with a ss into top of beginning ch-1. Fasten off.

ROUND 5: Join Ivory, ch 3 (counts as first dc), dc into each st to end. Join with a ss into top of beginning ch-3. Fasten off.

ROUND 6: Join Sable ch 1 (counts as first sc), sc into each st to end. Join with a ss into top of beginning ch-1.

ROUND 7: Ch 1 (counts as first sc), sc into each st to end. Join with a ss into top of beginning ch-1. Fasten off.

ROUND 8: Join Aguamarina, ch 3 (counts as first dc), dc into each st to end. Join with a ss into top of beginning ch-3. Fasten off.

ROUND 9: Join Sable, ch 1 (counts as first sc), sc into each st to end. Join with a ss into top of beginning ch-1.

ROUND 10: Ch 1 (counts as first sc), sc into each st to end. Join with a ss into top of beginning ch-1. Fasten off.

ROUND 11: Join Acanthe, ch 3 (counts as first dc), dc into each st to end. Join with a ss into top of beginning ch-3. Fasten off.

ROUND 12: Join Sable, ch 1 (counts as first sc), sc into each st to end. Join with a ss into top of beginning ch-1.

ROUND 13: Ch 1 (counts as first sc), sc into each st to end. Join with a ss into top of beginning ch-1. Fasten off.

ROUND 14: Join Ivory, ch 3 (counts as first dc), dc into each st to end. Join with a ss into top of beginning ch-3. Fasten off.

ROUND 15: Join Sable, ch 1 (counts as first sc), sc into each st to end. Join with a ss into top of beginning ch-1.

ROUND 16: Ch 1 (counts as first sc), sc into each st to end. Join with a ss into top of beginning ch-1. Fasten off.

ROUND 17: Join Blé, ch 3 (counts as first dc), dc into each st to end. Join with a ss into top of beginning ch-3. Fasten off.

ROUND 18: Join Sable, ch 1 (counts as first sc), sc into each st to end. Join with a ss into top of beginning ch-1.

ROUND 19: ch 1 (counts as first sc), sc into each st to end. Join with a ss into top of beginning ch-1. Fasten off.

ROUND 20: Join Rose Layette, ch 3 (counts as first dc), dc into each st to end. Join with a ss into top of beginning ch-3. Fasten off.

ROUND 21: Join Sable, ch 1 (counts as first sc), sc into each st to end. Join with a ss into top of beginning ch-1.

ROUND 22: ch 1 (counts as first sc), sc into each st to end. Join with a ss into top of beginning ch-1. Fasten off.

ROUND 23: Join Aguamarina, ch 3 (counts as first dc), dc into each st to end. Join with a ss into top of beginning ch-3. Fasten off.

ROUND 24: Join Sable, ch 1 (counts as first sc), sc into each st to end. Join with a ss into top of beginning ch-1.

ROUND 25: ch 1 (counts as first sc), sc into each st to end. Join with a ss into top of beginning ch-1. Fasten off.

ROUND 26: Join Acanthe, ch 3 (counts as first dc), dc into each st to end. Join with a ss into top of beginning ch-3. Fasten off.

ROUND 27: Join Sable, ch 1 (counts as first sc), sc into each st to end. Join with a ss into top of beginning ch-1.

ROUND 28: ch 1 (counts as first sc), sc into each st to end. Join with a ss into top of beginning ch-1. Fasten off.

ROUND 29: Join Blé, ch 3 (counts as first dc), dc into each st to end. Join with a ss into top of beginning ch-3. Fasten off.

ROUND 30: Join Sable, ch 1 (counts as first sc), sc into each st to end. Join with a ss into top of beginning ch-1.

ROUND 31: (Right hand) ch 1 (counts as first sc), sc into next 18 sts, ch 5, skip 5 sts, sc into next 6 sts. Join with a ss into top of beginning ch-1. Fasten off.
(Left hand) ch 1 (counts as first sc), sc into next 6 sts, ch 5, skip 5 sts, sc into next 18 sts. Join with a ss into top of beginning ch-1. Fasten off.

ROUND 32: Join Rose Layette, ch 1 (counts as first sc), sc into each st and also into thumb space of previous round. Join with a ss into top of beginning ch-1.

ROUND 33: ch 1 (counts as first sc), sc into each st to end. Join with a ss into top of beginning ch-1. Fasten off.

ROUND 34: Join Aguamarina, ch 1 (counts as first sc), sc into each st to end. Join with a ss into top of beginning ch-1. Fasten off

ROUND 35: Join Ivory, ch 1 (counts as first sc), sc into each st to end. Join with a ss into top of beginning ch-1.

ROUND 36: ch 1 (counts as first sc), sc into each st to end. Join with a ss into top of beginning ch-1. Fasten off.

ROUND 37: Join Safran, ch 1 (counts as first sc), sc into each st to end. Join with a ss into top of beginning ch-1. Fasten off.

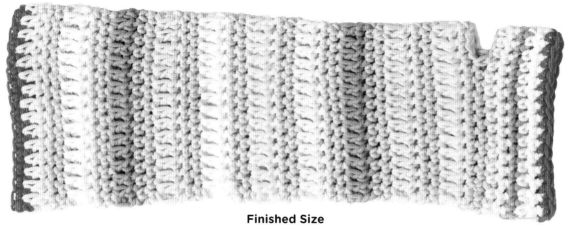

Finished Size
20 cm diameter / 25 cm length

Crochet Basics

Slip Knot

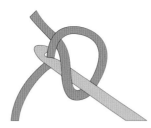 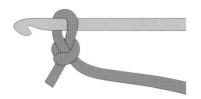

Create a loop with your yarn, making sure that the tail end is hanging behind your loop. Insert the hook through the loop, and pick up the ball end of the yarn.

Draw yarn through loop and pull on tail end gently to create slip knot on hook.

Chain

Nearly all crochet projects start with a series of chain stitches as well as being used within stitch patterns. It is important to keep your tension even so the stitches are neither too tight or too loose.

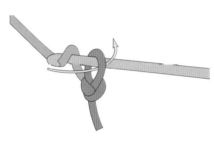

Start with a slip knot on your hook, wrap yarn over hook and draw through loop on hook to complete chain stitch.

Single Crochet
(sc)

This is the shortest of the crochet stitches and one of the easiest and most commonly used stitches.

Start by inserting your hook into the indicated chain or stitch. Wrap yarn over hook and draw through loop on hook. There are now 2 loops on the hook.

Wrap yarn over hook and draw through both loops to complete the stitch.

Double Crochet (dc)

This stitch is the other most commonly used stitch. It is a taller stitch that creates a softer, more open fabric.

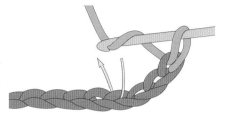

Start by wrapping yarn over hook before inserting it into your work. Wrap yarn over hook again

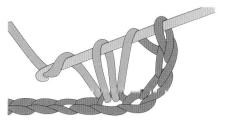

and draw loop through. You now have 3 loops on your hook. Wrap yarn over hook and draw through first 2 loops.

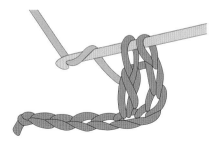

Wrap yarn over hook again and draw through both loops to complete the stitch

Half Double Crochet (hdc)

This stitch is halfway in height between a single crochet and double crochet.

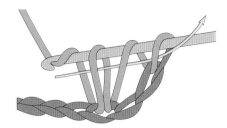

Start by wrapping yarn over hook before inserting it into your work. Wrap yarn over hook again and draw loop through. You now have 3 loops on your hook. Wrap yarn over hook and draw through all 3 loops to complete the stitch.

Treble
(tr)

This stitch is taller than double crochet and is often used in decorative stich patterns or to add height to corners.

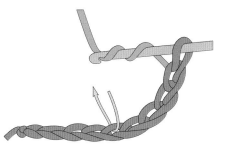

Start by wrapping yarn over hook twice before inserting it into your work.

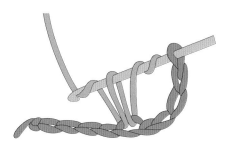

Wrap yarn over hook and draw loop through. You now have 4 loops on your hook.

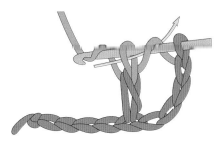

Wrap yarn over hook and draw through first 2 loops. You now have 3 loops on hook. Wrap yarn over hook and draw through 2 loops on hook. You now have 2 loops left.

Wrap yarn over and draw through remaining 2 loops to complete the stitch.

Abbreviations
(US Terms Used)

ch	chain
ss	slip stitch
sc	single crochet
dc	double crochet
tr	treble/triple crochet
st/s	stitch/es
sp/s	space/s
hdc	half double crochet
yo	yarn over
xdc	crossed double crochet
pc	popcorn st

Double Treble (dtr)
Triple Treble (ttr)

These stitches are worked in the same way as a treble stitch. The stitch height is altered by the amount of times you wrap the yarn around your hook at the beginning of the stitch.

A double treble is started by wrapping yarn over hook 3 times.

A triple treble is started by wrapping yarn over hook 4 times.

The stitch is then completed in the same way as a treble by wrapping yarn over hook and drawing through 2 loops at a time until the end.

Slip Stitch (ss)

This stitch does not add height to your work and is most commonly used to move to a different position or for joining.

To start, insert your hook into the indicated stitch. Yarn over hook and draw through both loops on hook to complete.

Blanket Stitch

Work from left to right. Bring needle up at 1, down at 2 and up at 3, keeping the thread looped under the needle. Pull thread through and shape stitch as desired. Repeat multiple stitches until complete.

Tips

For an even line of stitching keep the height of the stitches even throughout. To vary the look of the stitch, change the height of each stitch making one long and one short.

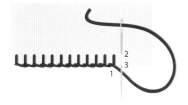

Shells

This stitch is most often used as a decorative scalloped border and is generally made using taller stitches such as double or treble crochet.

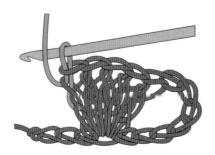

Shells are formed by working a number of stitches into the same point.

To make a shell, work the specified number of stitches into the same space.

Clusters

Clusters are the reverse of a shell in that a number of stitches are worked before joining together at the top. This creates a shell that fans out downwards.

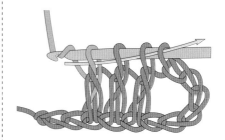

To make a double crochet cluster, work the stitch as normal but stopping at the final step of drawing yarn through last 2 loops. Keep these loops on your hook and start the next double crochet, in the next stitch but stopping before the final step. Continue working this way for the required amount of stitches.

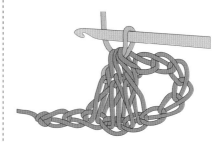

Once you have all your stitches made, yarn over hook and draw through all loops to complete cluster.

Bobbles

Bobbles are a textural stitch, giving your work a raised surface. They are worked in a similar way to a cluster except that all the stitches are worked into the same space.

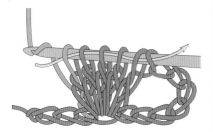

Work your stitches as normal but stop at the final step of drawing yarn through last 2 loops. Keep these loops on your hook and start the next double crochet, into the same stitch but stopping before the final step. Continue working this way until the required amount of stitches have been made.

Normally a bobble will be secured at the top by a chain stitch. However some patterns may specify not to complete this step. Always check your pattern whether this step is required.

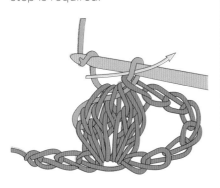

Puff Stitches

A puff stitch is similar to a bobble stitch but is made using half double crochet stitches and is smoother and plumper than a bobble.

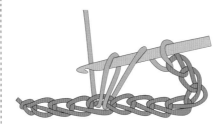

Start by making an incomplete half double crochet stitch (i.e. don't complete the final stage of drawing yarn through last 3 loops. When starting each new half double crochet, draw the loop up higher than you would normally.

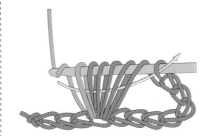

Once the required number of stitches have been made, draw yarn through all loops on hook.

Normally this stitch will be secured by a chain stitch. However this will vary according to the pattern. Check your pattern instructions first.

Popcorns

This stitch is similar to a shell but it is drawn together at the top to create surface texture.

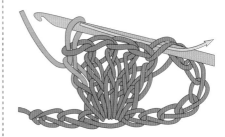

Work the required number of stitches into the same space. When the last stitch has been completed, remove hook and insert into the top of the first stitch of the group, pick up dropped loop.

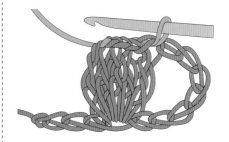

Yarn over hook, draw through both loops to complete.

The completed popcorn will sit away from the surface of your work.

DMC NATURA COLOUR PALETTE

In this book we only use DMC Natura Just Cotton,
here you can see the complete range of 60 colours.

N 01 Ibiza	N 26 Blue Jeans	N 30 Glicine
N 02 Ivory	N 28 Zaphire	N 88 Orléans
N 35 Nacar	N 27 Star Light	N 31 Malva
N 36 Gardenia	N 53 Blue Night	N 59 Prune
N 37 Canelle	N 49 Turquoise	N 45 Orquidea
N 78 Lin	N 64 Prussian	N 44 Agatha
N 39 Ombre	N 54 Green Smoke	N 80 Salomé
N 22 Tropic Brown	N 14 Green Valley	N 03 Sable
N 41 Siena	N 46 Forêt	N 83 Blé
N 86 Brique	N 38 Liquen	N 16 Tournesol
N 85 Giroflée	N 81 Acanthe	N 75 Moss Green
N 47 Safran	N 82 Lobelia	N 43 Golden Lemon
N 18 Coral	N 52 Geranium	N 74 Curry
N 23 Passion	N 07 Spring Rose	N 12 Light Green
N 34 Bourgogne	N 06 Rose Layette	N 79 Tilleul
N 87 Glacier	N 32 Rose Soraya	N 76 Bamboo
N 20 Jade	N 51 Erica	N 13 Pistache
N 25 Aguamarina	N 33 Amaranto	N 48 Chartreuse
N 05 Bleu Layette	N 62 Cerise	N 09 Gris Argent
N 56 Azur	N 61 Crimson	N 11 Noir